JOHN

Proclamation Commentaries

Jesus Christ in Matthew, Mark, and Luke,
Jack Dean Kingsbury

John, D. Moody Smith
(Second Edition, Revised and Enlarged)

Luke, Frederick W. Danker
(Second Edition, Revised and Enlarged)

Mark, Paul J. Achtemeier
(Second Edition, Revised and Enlarged)

Matthew, Jack Dean Kingsbury
(Second Edition, Revised and Enlarged)

Paul and His Letters, Leander E. Keck

PROCLAMATION COMMENTARIES

**Second Edition
Revised and Enlarged**   Gerhard Krodel, *Editor*

JOHN

D. Moody Smith

FORTRESS PRESS   PHILADELPHIA

COPYRIGHT © 1986 BY FORTRESS PRESS

Second printing 1987

Library of Congress Cataloging-in-Publication Data

Smith, D. Moody (Dwight Moody)
    John.

    (Proclamation commentaries)
    Bibliography: p.
    Includes index.
    1. Bible. N.T. John—Criticism, interpretation,
etc. I. Title. II. Series.
BS2615.2.S62   1986   226'.506   86-2035
ISBN 0-8006-1917-X

3267I87   Printed in the United States of America   1-1917

To
Cynthia
Catherine
David
Allen

CONTENTS

PREFACE

The invitation to revise the Proclamation Commentary on John makes it possible to expand the book in several respects and bring it up to date. There are essentially three major areas in which additions have been made: John and the synoptic Gospels; the relationship of the Gospel to the Johannine Epistles; and the new literary analysis of the Gospel. As the first edition owed a great deal to the insights of J. Louis Martyn and Raymond E. Brown concerning the synagogue controversy underlying the Gospel, insights which have by no means been superseded, this revision is indebted to Brown's later work on the Epistles and to R. Alan Culpepper's harvesting and harnessing of the results of modern narratological analysis for the interpretation of the Fourth Gospel. That such more recent work accommodates itself to the direction originally taken confirms that it was not ill-chosen. The work of Frans Neirynck and others on the relation of John to the synoptics has certainly demonstrated that any facile assertion of John's independence of the synoptics is no longer possible. Thus this problem receives much more serious attention.

The secretarial staff of the Divinity School, under Mrs. Frances Parrish's supervision, has responded promptly and competently to my needs. Judith Hill and Stephen Pogoloff, doctoral candidates at Duke, have made a new index and helped in other ways. I am grateful to them and to the reviewers, students, and other readers who have offered criticism, encouragement, and advice. The dedication of the first edition to our children is maintained. They continue to represent for us the goal and task of interpretation in preserving, transmitting, and translating the tradition and the message from one generation to the next.

D. Moody Smith
The Divinity School
Duke University

PART 1

INTRODUCTION

Biblical introduction in the classical, formal sense deals with questions of authorship, date, place of origin, language, structure, sources, intended readers, and purpose. There are questions that can only be answered after a careful study of the book in question, if at all. The original intention of biblical introduction was to resolve such questions so that the Bible might be read like any other literature. This laudable purpose has scarcely been fulfilled in the manner intended because of the difficulty in answering them.

Nowhere is the difficulty greater, or the questions more intriguing, than in the case of the Gospel of John. John's Gospel stands out sharply from the other canonical Gospels, but is similar in language and conceptuality to the three Johannine Epistles and has remarkable affinities with a variety of religions and religious texts of antiquity. To the questions: Who wrote it? When? For whom? To what ends? there have been many answers, some quite plausible. But a certain tantalizing aura of mystery hangs over the Gospel until today.

In this introduction we deal first with the relationship of the Gospel of John to the other canonical Gospels, the Johannine Epistles, and the wider religious world (Chapter 1). Then we turn to the structure or plot of the Gospel (Chapter 2), comparing it where appropriate to the other Gospels. The purpose is not so much to answer questions of introduction as to illumine them and thus to prepare for more extensive study of representative Johannine texts (Part II).

CHAPTER ONE

THE DISTINCTIVE CHARACTER
OF THE FOURTH GOSPEL

The Gospel of John is distinctive within the gospel canon. Matthew, Mark, and Luke see the ministry of Jesus together, in a similar perspective and framework, and are therefore called *synoptic* (from Greek words meaning "with" and "see"). Although they differ among themselves, the synoptics as a group can be contrasted with John on a number of important points. There is a sense in which John stands alone within the canon, unique and different from the other gospels in framework and content, yet sharing their narrative form.

Moreover, John belongs to a corpus of books traditionally ascribed to the same author. Three letters and an apocalypse are handed down to us in the NT as the work of the same John. Although there are stylistic, linguistic, and theological reasons for doubting common authorship of all the documents, there are some striking similarities among them, particularly between the Gospel and Epistles. The strong similarities between the Gospel and the Epistles were noted by the third-century bishop, Dionysius of Alexandria, who argued that they bespoke common authorship, while maintaining that the Book of Revelation could scarcely be the work of the same writer. His perception and arguments were sound, although it is now a live issue whether even the Gospel and Epistles come from the same hand. The Gospel's relation to the other Johannine writings is a significant matter. But of paramount importance are the characteristics and features which both tie the Fourth Gospel to the other three Gospels and distinguish it from them.

John and the Synoptic Gospels:
Similarities and Differences

Some of the similarities between John and the synoptics are striking. As in the synoptics, the first narrative of Jesus' ministry in John deals with his encounter with John the Baptist, who, incidentally, is not called "the Baptist" in John. Then comes a scene in which Jesus calls disciples who will go about with him. The public ministry begins in Galilee and consists principally of Jesus' miraculous deeds, mostly healings, his teachings and conversations, the opposition his ministry engenders, his arrest, trial, and death in Jerusalem, and the subsequent resurrection appearances to disciples in Galilee and Jerusalem. In the final Jerusalem period there is a last supper with the disciples, which plays an important role, and a long discourse or discourses addressed to them. The resurrection accounts begin with the discovery of the empty tomb. In these and other respects John parallels, or is similar to, the synoptic Gospels. Moreover, John contains a number of specific narratives that are clearly versions, or close relatives, of stories found in the synoptic Gospels: the cleansing of the temple, the healing of an official's son, the feeding of a multitude by the Sea of Galilee, Jesus' stilling a storm, the anointing of Jesus' feet by a woman, the triumphal entry into Jerusalem, Peter's betrayal, and others, particularly such as are a part of the passion or resurrection accounts of the synoptics.

Certain of these parallel narratives constitute structural elements common to John as well as to the synoptics: the opening reference to Jesus' baptism and the calling of disciples in Galilee; in the middle of the Gospel a feeding of a multitude and the stilling of a storm followed by the Johannine version of Peter's confession, all in Galilee; from that point onward mounting hostility to Jesus as he moves to Jerusalem; the entry into Jerusalem followed by the last supper, Jesus' final discourse with his disciples, the arrest, trial, crucifixion, burial, discovery of the empty tomb, and the resurrection appearances.

Common elements can be adduced in such numbers it is not surprising that throughout most of Christian history efforts have been made to synchronize or otherwise harmonize John with the other canonical Gospels. As far as we know, this effort began in earnest with Tatian's Diatessaron, a late second-century composite drawn from the canonical Gospels, and perhaps from other sources. It continues down to the present in imaginative, non-scientific books and films, not to mention sermons, about Jesus. Yet the task of combining John with the synoptics is not an easy one, and the attempts to do so have never been entirely plausible or convincing, despite the best efforts of ancient and subsequent authors. The reasons for this have to do with the differing character of the Johannine and synoptic accounts and of the material of which they are composed.

When one inquires about the differences between John and the synoptics he finds they are real, considerable, and have to do with more than inconsequential details. Although in John Jesus' ministry begins in Galilee, he quickly and repeatedly goes to Jerusalem; in fact, it is no exaggeration to say that his ministry is principally in Jerusalem. In the synoptic Gospels there is no visit to Jerusualem until the final week of his life. By the same token, there is only one Passover feast in the synoptics. There are three in John (2:13; 6:4; 11:55). According to the synoptics, Jesus' ministry could have been completed within a year. John's account requires between two and three years.

In the synoptic Gospels, Jesus is clearly presented as the Christ, the Jewish Messiah. Yet he appears within a Palestinian Jewish context rather than over against it. He is not a Christian *rather than* a Jew. In John, on the other hand, Jesus stands over against his Jewish interlocutors and opponents. If he is styled the king of Israel (1:49), he is nevertheless also the leader and lord of a Christian community distinct from "the Jews." Those who believe in or follow Jesus are generally distinguished from the Jews, who do not. Accordingly, in John Jesus speaks in Christian terms about himself. He argues with opponents about who he is; he expounds his messiahship and sonship in a way that is quite foreign to the synoptics. The style as well as the theology of the Johannine Jesus finds nearer echoes in 1 John than in the other Gospels.

Moreover, certain characteristics of Jesus' style and speech with which the synoptic Gospels have familiarized us are completely absent from John's Gospel. John contains no pronouncement stories, that is, no brief stories in which a problem or question is posed, to be answered or solved by a brief epigrammatic saying of Jesus (cf. Mark 2:23–28; 12:13–17). Nor are the sharp, earthy, and pithy sayings of Jesus, so well-known from the synoptics (cf. Luke 9:57–62; 6:19–21; 8:16–20), found in John. Rather Jesus speaks in a more elevated, hieratic, even pretentious, style. The parables of Jesus, virtually his pedagogical hallmark, are missing from John's Gospel. There are figures or allegories (John 10:1ff.; 15:1ff.), but they are unlike the synoptic parables of Jesus (cf. Mark 4:3–8, 26–29, 30–32; Luke 10:29–37; 15:11–24). Interestingly enough, the demon exorcisms (e.g., Mark 1:21–28), characteristic of Jesus' activity in Mark and the other synoptics (cf. Matt. 12:28/Luke 11:20), are, for reasons not immediately apparent, completely absent from John.

Not only Jesus' style of speech and activity, but the content of Jesus' teaching also differs, and often because of Johannine omission of synoptic characteristics. We have noted the Christian confessional themes of the discourses attributed to Jesus. Conversely, the characteristic synoptic theme of the kingdom of God and its coming (Mark 1:15) is missing from John. Jesus may speak of the kingdom (John 3), but not frequently, and not in the expectancy of its imminent appearance. Correspondingly, Jesus also speaks of himself as Son of man, but not of the coming apocalyptic Son of man familiar from the synoptics.

Specific narratives or other passages found in the synoptics are missing from John, and many Johannine narratives are not found in the synoptics. Missing from John are most of the (originally Markan) miracle stories (indeed, all the healings as well as the demon exorcisms), the synoptic parables, the infancy narratives, the transfiguration of Jesus, the institution of the Lord's Supper, the Sermon on the Mount, and the account of the trial of Jesus before the Sanhedrin. Among the Johannine narratives missing from the synoptics are the miracle of the transformation of the water into wine (2:1–11), Jesus' encounters with Nicodemus (John 3) and the Samaritan woman (John 4), the long conversation with Pilate at the trial (chaps. 18—19), and the raising of Lazarus (chap. 11). It is not inaccurate to say that most of the synoptic sayings and stories of Jesus are missing from John. The obverse is also the case;

most Johannine materials are not found in the synoptics. Occasionally, there is a widely variant Johannine parallel to a synoptic narrative (e.g., the encounter with John, the call of the disciples, the confession of Peter). Rarely, John has substantially the same narrative, but at a different place (e.g., the cleansing of the temple at the beginning of the ministry instead of in the passion week). But to an extent the ordinary Christian reader may no longer notice, the Fourth Gospel simply differs from the other three.

This basic situation may be stated as follows in terms of the widely accepted Markan hypothesis. Some Markan material, especially narrative, is closely paralleled in John. A small amount of Q material (common to Matthew and Luke only), mostly sayings, is paralleled in John. Almost no M (distinctly Matthean) material is found in John. Although little L (distinctly Lukan) material appears in the same form in John, there are nevertheless some striking points of similarity between these two Gospels only (e.g., the Baptist's denial that he is the Christ, the absence of a description of Jesus' baptism, the absence of a formal trial of Jesus before the Jerusalem Sanhedrin, etc.).

John's Gospel as a Problem in the Ancient Church and in Modern Criticism

The recognition that the differences between John and the synoptics constitute a difficulty to be explained is not a discovery of modern scholarship. The problem of John, or the Fourth Gospel, among the Gospels was recognized as such in the second century. There is evidence that John's Gospel was rejected by some Christians at that time, perhaps because it was being used by other Christians who were deemed heretical, but in part because it was different from, and seemed irreconcilable with, the synoptic Gospels, which were gaining universal acceptance among Christians.

Ancient Christian theologians and exegetes not only saw differences between John and the synoptics, but understood the problems that they raised. There was, first of all, a historical problem. John and the synoptics seem to disagree in their accounts of Jesus' ministry. Apparently, there grew up early a tradition of how to harmonize the disparate accounts so that all the events of each found a place. Tatian as early as 170 had composed the Diatessaron, the first such harmony of which we have knowledge. When, later in the second century Gaius of Rome objected to the Fourth Gospel, he pointed out that John was different from the other accounts (e.g., no temptation story!). Hippolytus acknowledged that this was the case, but argued John's account could be reconciled with the others.[1] So on all sides the problem was recognized. Early in the third century Origen (*Commentary on John*, 10, 2) pronounced all attempts to reconcile the various accounts, particularly the synoptic and Johannine, futile. For Origen they pointed to different or higher levels of meaning and were not to be leveled off for the sake of a specious historical uniformity.

Modern exegesis, on the basis of presuppositions and purposes different from Origen's (but with no sharper insight), has also rejected attempts to reconcile John and the synoptics at the historical level. That requires believing too many improbable things. Generally, the synoptic account is preferred, mainly because it is with good reason thought to represent more faithfully the forms, style, and subjects of Jesus' own actions and speech. Obviously, theological motifs are present in the structure and content of John, but this is also true of the others. Chronological considerations do not govern the structure or arrangement of the episodes of the synoptic Gospels except in the broadest sense. (Obviously Jesus' baptism by John preceded his trial.) John is no different in this respect. It may be the case that John has some things right in distinction from the synoptics. Jesus may have assumed a public role three years before his death. His last supper with his disciples may have taken place on Thursday just before Passover rather than on Passover eve Thursday. However that may be, the preference for the synoptics over John as a historical source for Jesus is not misplaced. John's differences are mainly the result of a thoroughgoing theological program presented in narrative form. John is not history "wie es eigentlich gewesen ist"—as it actually took place (Ranke).

John's relationship to the other Gospels is also a literary puzzle. Simply put, it is the question of why, given its similarities and wide divergences, the Fourth Gospel was written in the first place. As long as one thought that the Gospel was written by John the son of Zebedee at a ripe old age the answer was not difficult to come by. John had seen it all take place a long time before and had read the other accounts. He writes with them in view. His Gospel is a kind of meditation, authentic and apostolic, upon that distant and fading eyewitness. Robert Browning has given an imaginative poetic rendition of this classic position in "A Death in the Desert." Of course, that John's Gospel was the work of John the disciple of Jesus became the accepted and traditional position after Bishop Irenaeus of Lyons defended it in the late second century. Modern criticism seriously questions this position (pp. 72–74, below), but even if one accepts it the answer to the question of why John wrote as he did is finally not obvious. Why should the author narrate some things we otherwise know and omit others? What governs his choice of what he will tell and what he will omit?

In the second century the question of why John wrote such a different Gospel was apparently already asked. We do not see the question in extant sources so much as we hear some of the answers. In the early fourth century, Eusebius (*Ecclesiastical History* 6.14.7) theorized that John, knowing the other Gospels, had written down what Jesus did before John the Baptist was put into prison (3:24), while the synoptics record only what he did subsequently (Mark 1:14). There may be some truth in this theory, but it obviously will not work as a comprehensive explanation, since much of John overlaps with the synoptics. The ancient Muratorian fragment, which probably reflects the usage of the Roman church toward the end of the second century, speaks of John's having written after the other Gospels were in circulation and at the instance of his disciples. Perhaps the most eloquent explanation was given by Clement of Alexandria (*E. H.* 6.14.7), who wrote that John, recognizing that the other evangelists had written down the "bodily facts," wrote a "spiritual Gospel."[2] Clement's whole statement would repay thorough investigation and exegesis. For our purposes it suffices to observe that it has seemed so apposite to modern exegetes that it has found a place in many an introduction to the NT. Clement is clearly correct and to the point. He answers the question, "Why did John write?" in an appealing and satisfying way.

Modern criticism has for years accepted Clement's explanation, without buying into all that he presupposes about Johannine origins and authorship. Yet Clement's answer to the question of why John wrote is less satisfactory than at first appears. John emphasizes the importance of the Spirit for Jesus' followers, but at the same time insists that what he writes is attested by eyewitnesses of real events. It is not just symbolic or spiritual truth. Whether John, the author, himself would have accepted Clement's description as adequate is a fair question. Moreover, Clement, with Eusebius and the Muratorian fragment, assumes that the Fourth Evangelist knew the other, synoptic Gospels and wrote with full cognizance of them, approving them. But this answer to the question of why John wrote at least has apologetic overtones. For the purpose of those who accepted the Fourth Gospel as authoritative scripture, or who wanted to promote it as such, it was important to maintain that it was intended to complement and support the other Gospels, perhaps even to correct or clarify some details in them, not to contradict them.

Modern criticism has gone in several directions on the question of why John wrote such a different Gospel. Many scholars of the earlier half of the century, and some still today, accept at least this much of the ancient tradition. John wrote with the other Gospels in view to interpret or supplement them. Admittedly most no longer feel compelled to defend John's historicity where it diverges from the others. But even this concession to critical insights may not account for why John writes as he does, so independently, yet with some regard for a common pattern we know from other Gospels. "John is a text without commentary," wrote Hans Windisch more than a half-century ago.[3] In Windisch's view John wished to displace the text with his commentary. He wrote in order to supplant the other Gospels with one that did justice to the divine reality he saw manifest in Jesus. Perhaps with tongue in cheek Windisch put on the back of his title page in Greek—so that the uninitiated might not read and be offended—2 Cor. 5:16 and John 5:8: "If we once knew Christ according to the flesh we know him so no longer" and "All that came before me are thieves and robbers." John wishes to write a wholly spiritual and theological Gospel and with it to displace in church usage the synoptics and any other competing Gospel.

This sounds like a radical solution, but maybe it is not. After emphasizing his radicality, Windisch points out that what he is suggesting is, after all, not unprecedented in the development of biblical literature. The Chronicler probably wrote his history of the Israelite kingship to displace what we find in Samuel and Kings. Matthew incorporates over ninety percent of Mark, and did not intend that his readers should know and use Mark as well. Luke states that he intended to put forward an orderly account, implying that his predecessors' work was inadequate. Probably each of our Gospels was at one point the Gospel for one church or Christian community. To have one Gospel was simpler. Two, three, or finally four introduce complexities. When Tatian took the four in use in the second half of the second century and combined them into one he was reverting to the more ancient practice of the church, and his Diatessaron held sway in the Syrian church for centuries.

That John wrote to displace the other Gospels is difficult to prove, but remains a plausible theory, given the Fourth Gospel's radical differences from the other three. But this radical solution to the Johannine puzzle invites another, perhaps equally radical. What if John wrote in relative or complete ignorance of the other Gospels? What if the similarities are to be accounted for by the common pool of information or tradition that any Christian writer of the latter part of the first century would have shared? The vast differences are then simply the product of John's having inhabited some different, more remote, corner of the Christian world.

Percival Gardner-Smith advanced this proposal shortly before World War II.[4] Gardner-Smith's thesis, if correct, completely undercuts Windisch's. You cannot intend to displace what you do not know. Yet Windisch's name is never mentioned in Gardner-Smith's slim book, although Windisch had published more than a decade earlier. Had Gardner-Smith never heard of Windisch? Unlikely. More probably this is a Cambridge don's way of dealing with a German he wishes to dispose of—ignore him. Gardner-Smith convinced his distinguished colleague C. H. Dodd, whose works on the Fourth Gospel were widely influential.[5] On the continent Rudolf Bultmann had already rejected Windisch and wrote his commentary (1941) on the assumption of John's independence of the synoptics.[6] With various permutations the thesis of John's independence is now so widely held that it is now being contested as the reigning view. It is still the inclination of most interpreters, however, to see John as an independent Gospel—independent of the other three. Otherwise, Windisch's claim that the Fourth Evangelist wrote with an eye to displacing the other Gospels must be taken very seriously.

A third puzzle is the theological one. Windisch saw quite clearly that John's Gospel presents a picture of Jesus quite different from the other three. That they now stand together in the NT does not necessarily mean that in the beginning they formed a united front. In all probability they testify to the diversity of theological and other views canonized in the NT.

The second century of Christianity is a relatively obscure period. Most of the NT books were written during the first century or soon thereafter. The canon of Christian scripture had begun to take shape by the end of the second century. It is clear that Matthew, Mark, and Luke were used by many Christians throughout the century. John's Gospel, or traditions incorporated into it, was known to Ignatius of Antioch in the first two decades of the second century. Probably Justin Martyr at mid-century knew the Gospel, although he refers to it sparingly. His contemporary Marcion, who rejected the OT and was soon denounced for his heresies, apparently did not know it. Yet the Gospel of John was known and used by Valentinian Gnostic Christians in Rome. The Gospel of Truth, perhaps written by Valentinus, is steeped in Johannine language and conceptuality. The first known commentary on John was written by the Valentinian Gnostic Heracleon at mid-second century, although Irenaeus vigorously disputed the accuracy of Gnostic exegesis.[7] Montanists based their claim to incarnate the Spirit on Jesus' promise of the Paraclete in John's Gospel. Not surprisingly, conservative Roman Christians like Gaius refused to acknowledge the Fourth Gospel, despite claims of apostolic authorship already being made for it.[8]

Where do the theological roots of the Gospel of John lie? Not surprisingly John has been described as a Gnostic Gospel, or a Gospel written under Gnostic influence, perhaps opposed to Gnosticism. Many Johannine concepts— logos, light and darkness, God and the world—have their Gnostic counterparts. Whether John originated in Gnostic circles or was early adopted by Gnostics is an unsettled issue. Probably the latter is closer to the truth, but in any case John's early Gnostic connections are real and significant. The so-called Alogoi, who rejected the Fourth Gospel as incompatible with the others, had a point.

Yet one might contend that John after all makes no claims about Jesus that are opposed to what is found in the synoptics. Mark, for example, begins and ends his account of Jesus' ministry with solemn statements that Jesus is the Son of God. Yet in John it is Jesus who is always making those claims on his own behalf. True, Jesus also commands his disciples to love in John, as he does in all the Gospels. But whereas in the other Gospels he commands them to love their neighbors and even their enemies, in John he commands them to love one another, that is, other Christians. The circle of love seems confined to those who share the same belief in Jesus. Mutual love is the community's witness to, or against, the world of its loyalty to Jesus.

When at the end of the second century John began to be accepted by Christians generally as authoritative scripture, its Christology and ethics were reconciled with the synoptics, as well as with other Christian tradition, and vice versa. Nevertheless, the tensions remained and they remain still. Perhaps ironically, the Fourth Gospel played a large role in the later development of Christian doctrine. The deliberations and credal formulations of the great ecumenical councils of the fourth and fifth centuries are virtually inconceivable apart from the Fourth Gospel. The Fourth Gospel became the great pillar and biblical source of the forces of developing orthodoxy as expressed in the creeds. That is exactly where the irony lies. John's Gospel was itself questioned because it was used by parties whose doctrine was suspect, gave rise to charismatic excesses, and differed sharply from the other, accepted Gospels. Yet in time it became the very basis and standard of orthodoxy for the catholic church.

Modern NT exegesis has been aware of this irony for some time. Ernst Käsemann, a leading figure among the generation of German scholars who assumed university positions in the years following World War II, has put the matter with characteristic sharpness. The Gospel of John, he writes, was canonized by the providence of God and the error of man.[9] Käsemann said what many scholars have thought for a century or more. John's distinctive, dogmatic emphases and other sharp differences were honed down or harmonized to bring it into harmony with the synoptic Gospels. And the others were read in light of its pervasive Christology.

Käsemann may have overdrawn the difference in order to emphasize the point, but it is nevertheless real. Of course, the magnitude of the difference and its significance are related to the historical question of whether or not John wrote with the other Gospels in view. It was the opinion of the early church leaders who testify on the Gospel's behalf that he did, and that is not impossible. Yet, as we have observed, there are some problems with that position, particularly if one does not begin with it. That is, if one looks at the Gospel of John with a view to understanding its purpose and nature only, it is not immediately obvious that it was written to be read with other Gospels. As evidence has mounted that John was not necessarily written much later than the synoptics, the assumption that John must have known them has seemed less compelling. Interestingly enough, it is church tradition that suggests the composition of John came late, in Ephesus, possibly near the end of the first century (*E.H.* 3.23.1–4). The view that John was written early, perhaps on Palestinian soil, is the child of modern criticism. Obviously the fact that a tradition is congenial with a widely held opinion or with the interests of an institution does not mean it is false. Nevertheless, it is important to remember that the view that John wrote independently, or without intending to make his presentation amenable to the synoptics, would on historical grounds count heavily against the effort to see John as compatible with the other Gospels.

It may be that John knew the synoptics (or other Gospels), but it is not possible to prove that he did. Clearly he knew a number of narratives, especially a passion narrative, which we know from the synoptic Gospels. Obviously such similarities should be noted in the exegesis of the Fourth Gospel. But even if John knew those other Gospels, it is difficult to argue that he wrote primarily with them in view. Where John's narratives parallel the synoptics (usually and especially the Markan) the details differ, more often than not in unaccountable ways, and he does not seem to be dependent on any one of them. The attempt to account for John's rendition of a specific narrative on the hypothesis that he had a synoptic version before him and was deliberately employing and changing it often leads to tortuous exegesis. Nor has it been possible to explain comprehensively and convincingly the presence of some synoptic narratives and other materials and the absence of others by reference to a systematic intention to alter the synoptics. Recent research is at best ambiguous on the question of whether John knew the synoptics at all, and it is widely agreed that the possible relationship to them does not offer a broad avenue for the development of Johannine exegesis.

The Johannine Literature: The Gospel, the Epistles, and Revelation

Since stylistic, linguistic, and theological kinship between the Gospel and Epistles of John has been recognized since antiquity (see above, p. 2), the tradition of common authorship has quite naturally become well established and widely accepted. Whether or not it is strictly correct is now a debated question, and we shall in due course review some of the reasons for the debate. But, regardless of how that issue may be decided, their kinship is real and significant.

The very existence of letters implies that there was a community or group of churches which had a sense of sharing a common origin and destiny (1 John 1:1-4, 5; 3:2, 11). Moreover, the question of leadership within and among these churches (3 John 9-10), as well as that of doctrine (1 John 2:22-23; 4:2-3; 2 John 7-11) and authority (cf. 1 John 1:5; 3:11; and 4:1), appears to have become acute. If, as is now deemed possible, more than one author wrote the Gospel and letters, that is evidence of a common mode of speaking and thinking theologically that defined this community. The Johannine letters are traditionally regarded as catholic Epistles, in that they seem to address all Christians. There is a sense in which they have done just that and their message is in large measure appropriate for all. Thus the traditional way of reading them is not entirely off base. Yet in the beginning (to use the Johannine phrase) they sprang from and were addressed to specific Christians and Christian groups.

Because of the similarities between the Fourth Gospel and the letters it has long been customary to read the Gospel in light of the letters and vice versa. That is not illegitimate or misleading, and may well be what was originally intended, yet this should be done with caution, for there are significant differences as well as a broad base of similarities between them.

The similarities are obvious enough and extend to the choice of words and the structure of sentences. The presentation of Jesus Christ as word, light, and life stands out among a host of theological and terminological relationships. The fact that Christ as light and life stands opposed to darkness and death characterizes what has come to be known as the Johannine dualism, in which the images of salvation are paired with their opposites. All of this and more is distinctly, if not uniquely, Johannine. Moreover, the similarities of omission, while more subtle, are clear. It may not be significant that Jesus' Words of Institution of the Lord's Supper are missing from both Gospel and letters, although they are strikingly present in Paul (1 Cor. 11:22–25) as well as each of the synoptic Gospels. But Jesus' rich variety of specific injunctions, wisdom sayings, and commands known to us from the synoptic Gospels are in both Gospel and letters reduced to the single command to love. The scope of that love is, as we have noted, the circle of Jesus' disciples or the church. In neither do we find the command to love the enemy (Matt. 5:44; Rom. 12:20) or the neighbor (Lev. 19:19; Mark 12:31; Rom. 13:9; Gal. 5:14). The omission is clearly related to the Johannine dualism, in which the world plays a decidedly negative role, and the fellow Christian rather than the neighbor is the object of immediate concern. God loves the world (John 3:16) as the object of his salvation in Jesus Christ, but the world resists and even hates Jesus and his disciples (John 15:18–19). In the letters Christians are warned away from the world (1 John 2:15–17). John might have accepted the injunction to love the neighbor, if he had known it, but for the same or related reasons does not emphasize it.

The world is passing away (1 John 2:17), but those who are in the light (i.e., the love for one another inculcated by Jesus) will not fear its dissolution. To be in the light is to live in the world to come—a term which John, however, does not use—rather than in the darkness of that world that is passing away (1 John 2:8–11). In 1 John as in the Gospel the reality of salvation, that is, eternal life, is conceived as already available and present to faith. When Martha hopes for her brother Lazarus' resurrection at the last day, Jesus responds (11:25), "I am the resurrection and the life." Later Jesus deals with the question of how he himself will appear to the disciples and not (in accord with apocalyptic expectation) to the world (John 14:22–25). Thus, in John's Gospel we see at points a thoroughgoing realized eschatology. In the Epistles there is certainly an awareness that the eschatological salvation or life is being realized. The expectation of Jesus' return seems, however, livelier and more significant (1 John 2:18; 2:28; 3:2; 4:17). Exegetes generally recognize a difference of eschatological emphasis between the Gospel and the Epistles.

There are other differences. In the Gospel the widely prevalent early Christian understanding of Jesus' death as a sacrifice for sin is scarcely present at all (1:29), whereas in the letters (and Revelation) it is prominent (1 John 1:7–9; 2:2). In this as in other ways 1 John seems more traditional or tradition-oriented than the Gospel. In fact, this orientation to tradition is evident in the way the phrase "from the beginning" appears in 1 John (e.g., 1:1; 3:11). In the Gospel "the beginning" (Greek, *arche*) refers to the cosmic beginning, even before creation. In 1 John it clearly refers to the beginning from which the Christian message springs, that is, Jesus.[10] The author of 1 John wants to maintain that the message he is conveying and endorsing is the original one, in the most positive and significant sense of the term. Thus in speaking of the commandment of love which Jesus has given (2:7-8) he calls it the old commandment as well as the new commandment (cf. John 13:34), underscoring its traditional, and therefore authoritative, character.

The presentation of the Spirit is much less developed, it seems, in 1 John than in the Gospel. The term "Counselor" (Greek, *parakletos*, one "called to the side of") is found only of Jesus in 1 John (2:1, where it is translated "Advocate"). The idea of the Spirit-Paraclete as one who continues and even expands upon the revelation given by the historical Jesus, developed in the so-called paraclete-sayings of John 14—16, is missing in the letters. It may be that it had not yet developed. On the other hand, it is equally conceivable that it takes a back seat because of claims made by opponents in the name or on the authority of the Spirit (1 John 4:1). After all, who is to validate, or to deny, the claim and authority of one claiming to be inspired by the Spirit? Spirit inspiration was a significant phenomenon in the early church (Rev. 1:10), and apparently a problematic one (1 Cor. 12:3, as well as 1 John 4:1).

The fewer references to the Spirit in 1 John, which suggest either a more primitive stage of development or the deliberate avoidance of a problematic theme, raise the wider question of the chronological ordering of the Gospel and Epistles. Which came earlier? (Of course, it is not necessarily the case that the letters were written in the order in which they appear or that they were *all* written either before or after the Gospel.) The greater prominence of futuristic, apocalyptic eschatology in 1 John, the frequent invoking of tradition, the role of the sacrificial character of Jesus' death might also suggest that the letters, or at least 1 John, were written prior to the Gospel. On the other hand, the Gospel is logically prior to the letters and thus stands before them in the NT because it deals with Jesus who is historically, logically, and theologically prior.

Other factors may also point in the same direction. In the Gospel Jesus' opponents are described as Jews. The main issue is whether or not he is whom he claims to be and the question is whether they will believe. The OT, and especially OT figures, appear frequently. In the letters the Jewish opponents have disappeared; at least they are not named. The OT is alluded to but once and never quoted. Instead, the opponents seem to be other Christians and the problem is a christological one, namely that there are Christians who in some sense deny Jesus' fleshliness, his human reality. (Those who are said to deny that Jesus is the Christ in 2:22 may be the same people; in any case they are not called Jews.) At many points the teaching of the Gospel is assumed (e.g., the love commandment, the epistolary prologue), suggesting that the author presupposes it, whether in the form of the Fourth Gospel or in some earlier stage. In fact, in his commentary on the Epistles Raymond E. Brown has forcefully argued that they not only presuppose something like our Gospel, but that 1 John in particular is intended to establish the proper meaning and interpretation of the Gospel.[11] On his reading the opponents mentioned in 1 John are people who base themselves upon and promote an erroneous interpretation of the teaching of the Gospel. Obviously, no interpretation of the Gospel of John as a whole can lose sight of its close relation to the letters and the assumptions about origins and traditions which are found there. At the same time the points of contact with the synoptic Gospels, as well as the differences from them, are significant and cannot be ignored. What does it all add up to? We can make a provisional statement.

Probably John's Gospel is the distillation of the theological perspective of a Christian community which had access to a body of tradition about Jesus. That tradition had, however, been much more freely shaped to conform it to the community's beliefs than in the case of the synoptic Gospels. That such a community and tradition existed can be amply supported from the Gospel itself, but it is confirmed and strengthened by the Johannine Epistles, which give clear indication of the existence of more than one church within the orbit of a single leader, tradition, and theological perspective. The letters also betray the kinds of church-political and theological problems that stirred those churches and perhaps played some role in the formation, composition, and editing of our Gospel or its constitutive tradition. We shall deal more directly with the nature and interests of this form of Christianity in Chapter 7.

What then of the Apocalypse, the Revelation to John? Dionysius long ago saw that it could scarcely be ascribed to the same author as the Gospel and Epistles. Language, style, and theology are obviously quite different. The Greek of Revelation is frequently described as barbarous or the like, while that of the Gospel and Epistles is simple but elegant. The theology seems to be dominated by what modern interpreters have come to call apocalyptic. When at the end (22:20) Jesus says, "Surely I am coming soon," this seems to catch up the temper and import of the entire book. Nothing could be further from the realized eschatology of the Fourth Gospel, or so it seems. Also, the doctrine of the vicarious atonement by Jesus' blood plays an important role, in contrast to the Gospel. Yet there are between them some amazing points of contact or similarity. Both emphasize the importance of witnessing and attest the hostility of the world. Only in the Apocalypse is Jesus called the Word of God (in the Gospel "the word"; in 1 John "the word of life"). Only in the Book of Revelation (1:7) and the Gospel (19:34–35) does the piercing of Jesus play a role, in both cases based on Zech. 12:10. As if to fulfill Jesus' promise of the Paraclete, the Book of Revelation is itself apparently given through or by the Spirit, and the Spirit's speaking in chapters 1—3 is scarcely distinguished from the heavenly Jesus'. When Jesus speaks in Revelation, he utters "I am" sayings, as in the Gospel, or speaks in a manner reminiscent of the Gospel (3:20). But if, as in the Johannine letters, scripture is rarely if ever cited as such, the resemblance could not be more superficial. Revelation is in large part composed of OT material, especially the words of the prophets, although they are not cited or named. The OT is similarly important in the Gospel of John, although used in different ways.

While we cannot presuppose common authorship, the traditional connection of the Book of Revelation with the Gospel and Epistles of John is more than just an ancient mistake based on the fact that the author of Revelation was clearly someone named John (Rev. 1:1, 4, 9; 22:8). (Incidentally, it is the only Johannine book that names its author John, or names him at all. The Gospel is ascribed to a beloved disciple only, and 2 and 3 John to an elder.) Probably there is an actual historical relationship of some sort underlying the traditional linking of the Apocalypse to the other Johannine writings. What that relationship is we may never know precisely. In the meantime Revelation will scarcely be a major factor in the interpretation of the Fourth Gospel. It lies at the periphery, but it is nevertheless there, a distant relative if not a close cousin.

The Johannine Milieu

Even when John's knowledge of the synoptics has been taken for granted, the interpretation of the Fourth Gospel has required some other means of explaining its unusual character. The view that John's distinctiveness stems from Pauline influence was once widely held. Yet it grew less convincing as it became evident that for the most part Paul and John have in common just such theological ideas as they share with a broad spectrum of early Christianity. Much that is distinctive of Pauline terminology and thought does not appear in John and vice versa.

At one time, however, Paul and John were regarded as successive stages in the hellenization of early Christian experience, life, and thought. Albert Schweitzer, who opened a new epoch of Pauline interpretation by arguing that Paul's Christ mysticism was apocalyptic rather than Hellenistic in origin and character, nevertheless continued to view John's mysticism as Hellenistic. It represented, so to speak, a step beyond Paul. Schweitzer and others were surely correct in seeing in John a certain profound theological kinship to the Apostle to the Gentiles. Moreover, the sensibility that this kinship involved "mysticism" or the language of indwelling or participation was similarly correct. Bultmann saw the relationship primarily as a perception common to both Paul and John—that the eschatological reality had broken into the present—and he was accurate, although he was looking at a different aspect of Pauline and Johannine thought. In fact, Schweitzer and Bultmann actually agreed that eschatology was important for Paul and that John was significantly different from him. They differed in that Schweitzer continued to assume John's knowledge of Paul, or Pauline thought, while Bultmann no longer found this assumption necessary.[12] Although Bultmann refused to regard John as a development of specifically Pauline thought and did not think of John as representing an advance in the hellenization of Christianity, he continued to assume that John was a step farther removed than Paul from the primitive preaching and its originative center. He thought of this removal as a result of the increasing influence of Gnostic thought and spirit, as well as the so-called redeemer myth which Paul also knew. Yet the Gnostic influence as Bultmann conceived it was not more Hellenistic than Jewish. In his commentary on John, Bultmann spoke of a Gnosticism under OT influence, and when the Qumran Scrolls were discovered he took them to support his position. Moreover, he perceived John as rejecting the extremes of Gnostic thought. In occasional asides he allowed for the possibility that John's Gospel had actually arisen in a Jewish milieu out of a Christian tradition extending back to Jesus and the Baptist, but such considerations never loomed large in his interpretation of the Fourth Gospel.[13]

In the meantime, following Schweitzer's breakthrough, the interpretation of Paul was moving in a Jewish direction, typified by the work of W. D. Davies.[14] Davies argued that much in Paul that had been attributed to Hellenistic religion could in fact be explained out of his Judaism. Subsequently, the Scrolls were held to be relevant for understanding Paul as well. With the increasing recognition of such Jewish elements in Paul, and eventually in John, went the realization that Judaism and Hellenism were not locked in watertight compartments, so that a John or a Paul might have developed in one sphere but not the other. Instead, Judaism lived in a hellenized world in the first century, even in Palestine. The degree and strength of this hellenization may have varied from place to place or under changing political or cultural conditions, but it was always a factor to be reckoned with. There is a sense in which the recognition of the pervasive hellenization of Judaism runs parallel with Bultmann's view of a Gnosticism arising at the boundaries of Judaism rather than as an extreme hellenization of Christianity. They are not the same, but they are nonetheless analogous attempts to accommodate much of the same data arising out of the confluence of Judaism and surrounding cultures.

Doubtless the discovery, shortly after World War II, of the Qumran Scrolls of the Jewish Essene sect, as well as Nag Hammadi Gnostic documents, played a major role in showing how complex and interwoven were the tapestries of ancient Near Eastern religion. The Scrolls contained terminology and a dualism once thought to be Hellenistic. The Gnostic writings showed pre-Christian relationships to Judaism. Jewish, Hellenistic, and even Gnostic, were shown not be contradictory or mutually exclusive categories. (Although any Gnosticism that involves the rejection of creation or of the OT is no longer Jewish, a Jewish matrix of nascent Gnosticism is not thereby excluded.) Such labels or categories are largely scholarly conveniences. They point to something real but do not do justice to the actual mix of religious and cultural reality. There are Jewish, Hellenistic, and Gnostic elements or aspects of the Fourth Gospel. Exactly how they are to be defined is a matter of scholarly dispute.

For example, John is certainly Gnostic, at least in that knowing is an important dimension of believing in John. Further, terms (e.g., light, darkness, word) that are important in Gnosticism appear also in John. Certainly the Gospel flourished among Gnostic Christians in the second century and quickly made its way among gentile Christians in the Greco-Roman, that is, Hellenistic, world. John demands consideration as a document that was Gnostic and Hellenistic, at least in its use and interpretation, whatever may be the case of its origin.

At the same time the Fourth Gospel is significantly Jewish. That is, it enshrines an important and central relationship to Judaism, albeit not an altogether positive one. That John is years, decades, removed from Jesus and the most primitive church, that it differs sharply from the synoptics, or that it cannot be adequately explained as a development of Pauline thought does not mean that its relations to Jesus and the primitive church, to the synoptics, and to Paul are unreal or insignificant. Yet its pronounced Jewish dimension is not simply mediated through Jesus or the primitive church, any more than it is derived from the other Gospels or from Paul's letters. John has a definite profile in relation to Judaism which is distinct from that of other NT books and which gives to the Fourth Gospel much of its unique character. It will be worthwhile to notice some of the salient features of this profile before proceeding further.

John uses the OT in a positive way, as do all the Gospels. In fact, John's use of the OT frequently runs parallel to that of the synoptics (e.g., in the Baptist narrative at the beginning of the Gospel, at Jesus' entry into Jerusalem, at points in the passion narrative). Yet there is another entire dimension of John's appropriation of the OT. Jesus is directly or indirectly compared with OT figures, especially Moses (1:17), but also Jacob (4:12) and Abraham (8:53). Whether Moses had already given the children of Israel the true bread from heaven in the form of the manna in the wilderness or that bread is God's gift in Jesus is discussed at great length in Chapter 6. In John's view, of course, the latter is emphatically the case. Although the OT is unequivocally cited as authoritative scripture, it now is viewed as testimony to Jesus (1:45; 5:39). Whoever does not see that does not truly understand scripture and thus remains a Jew. When Jesus in John speaks of the law as "your law" (8:17) he means the law as it is fundamentally misunderstood (cf. 7:19) by those who do not believe in him.

So in John's Gospel, unlike the others (and unlike Paul), Jesus and his disciples are distinguished from "the Jews" (cf. 9:28). In the synoptic tradition the context within which Jesus appears is Jewish; he stands out in that context but does not stand outside it. This is accurate historically. John, on the other hand, is unhistorical or anachronistic in that his portrayal does not correspond to the situation of Jesus' own time and ministry. To put matters boldly, Jesus did not consider himself anything other than a Jew, and his summons to discipleship was not a call to cease being a Jew and become a Christian. In John's Gospel, however, that is in effect what becoming a disciple of Jesus means. The reasons for this are complex, and doubtless have to do with the historical setting of the Gospel vis-à-vis Judaism rather than with that of Jesus. Exactly what that situation is will become clearer as we look at specific Johannine texts and try to place them in historical contexts. Apparently John's unique focus and concentration on the question of who Jesus is has something to tell us about Jewish opposition to his understanding and presentation of Jesus.

John knows a great deal about Judaism. He knows Jewish feasts, traditions, and terms (which he sometimes translates for non-Jewish readers). Even his characteristic language and dualism have precedent in Jewish literature, especially the Qumran Scrolls, although that language was once described as philosophical and therefore Hellenistic. Certainly John is no more philosophical in his conceptuality and mindset than his great Jewish contemporary Philo of Alexandria (who was greatly influenced by Greek philosophy). In fact, he is probably much less so, and more deliberately oriented toward historical events per se.

Earlier quests for the religious background of the Johannine literature, ranging from Hellenistic philosophy to the mystery religions, even to Buddhism, and more recently to Mandaeism and Gnosticism, have at the very least had the merit of showing the widespread affinities of the religious language, symbolism, and experience represented in the Fourth Gospel. In recent years, however, a Jewish interaction with Johannine Christianity has increasingly been regarded as the proximate background and seedbed of the Fourth Gospel. (Such an interaction likely began as a dispute between Jews who believed Jesus was Messiah and those who did not.) This has come about not only as a result of a recognition of the number of such Jewish features and connections in the Fourth Gospel as we have observed, but also because of a growing awareness of the varieties of religious forms and expressions within Judaism during the NT period. Important aspects of many religions or religious currents of the first century found some representation in first-century Judaism. This dual recognition or phenomenon has encouraged and rewarded scholars interested in the Jewish milieu of the Fourth Gospel and Johannine Christianity.

CHAPTER TWO

THE STRUCTURE OF THE FOURTH GOSPEL

The exegesis of any text must take account of its position and role in the document of which it is a part. Thus exegesis of Johannine texts must keep the structure of the Fourth Gospel in view. As we have seen, a part of the distinctiveness of the Fourth Gospel is its difference in structure from the synoptics. Yet, although the itinerary of Jesus according to John differs from that of the synoptics, there is a general similarity in the pattern or structure of the Gospels. In John, as in the synoptics, a public ministry (John 2—12) is followed by a final Jerusalem period in which Jesus appears principally with his disciples (John 13—20). The differences are, of course, significant. In the synoptics Jesus seems to work for only a year or less in Galilee until the final journey to Jerusalem. In John he moves between Galilee and Jerusalem over a period of two to three years. In John Jesus no longer teaches publicly during the final Jerusalem period. In the synoptics he teaches publicly in Jerusalem, but only in a conflict situation (Mark 12; Matthew 23). In either case, Jesus' public ministry, and thus any effort to win wide support among the people, seems to have concluded as he turns to the cross.

In addition to the two major parts of the Gospel which we have noted, there is an introductory chapter and an appendix (chap. 21). The introduction consists of two distinct sections. The famous prologue (1:1–18) is followed by a long scene in which Jesus is, so to speak, introduced by John the Baptist (1:19–51). That Jesus was baptized by John is either ignored or presupposed. The descent of the Spirit upon Jesus as a dove (cf. Mark 1:10 parr.), which in the synoptics occurs at the baptism, is reported by John the Baptist. John, rather than the voice from heaven, pronounces Jesus Son of God. We do not read that Jesus was actually baptized by John. (There is an interesting similarity to Luke, who in 3:21 mentions that Jesus had been baptized, but gives no straightforward report of the baptism.) Very likely the Evangelist knew the tradition of Jesus' baptism by John the Baptist, but did not report it because of his desire clearly to subordinate John to Jesus. In Matthew's Gospel also Jesus' baptism by John seems to be a problem, for Matthew reports that John at first declines to baptize Jesus, saying that the roles should be reversed, until Jesus finally insists that he do so.

The encounter of Jesus and John (vv. 29ff.) leads directly to the rather long scene (1:35–51) in which Jesus gathers disciples. At first John sends two of his own disciples to Jesus (1:35–36). One of them, Andrew, then finds Peter his brother (1:40–42). Afterward, Jesus finds Philip and issues the invitation or command so familiar from the synoptic call stories, "Follow me" (1:43). At the end of the scene Jesus has five disciples. The twelve have not yet been mentioned, although they later enter the picture (6:67–71).

The Public Ministry

The stage is now set for the public ministry of Jesus, which begins with the wine miracle at Cana (2:1–11) and the cleansing of the temple in Jerusalem (2:13–22). It is not by coincidence that these stories appear at the beginning of John's rendition of Jesus' ministry. Both are epiphany stories, that is, narratives in which Jesus reveals or manifests himself. This characteristic is made quite explicit in 2:11: ". . . Jesus . . . manifested his glory, and his disciples believed in him." There is no synoptic parallel to the wine miracle. The story of the cleansing of the temple, which appears in the passion week according to the synoptic accounts, is moved forward by John to the beginning of Jesus' public ministry. Probably the synoptic positioning of the account is closer to historical fact, as it is intrinsically unlikely that Jesus performed this unusual act twice. In its Johannine setting the temple narrative shows Jesus at the very beginning of his ministry in confrontation with the Jewish authorities who will eventually do him in. The Johannine story itself concludes with a covert reference to Jesus' resurrection and, by implication, his crucifixion (2:19–22). The enigmatic sayings of Jesus, which his opponents typically do not understand, imply that Jesus himself will replace the temple as the proper center of worship (cf. 4:20–24). Already in these two introductory stories the character of Jesus' ministry is suggested. He is the giver of wine, the life-giving fluid. Thus he becomes the source of life (cf. 4:13–15). At the same time, he fulfills and displaces the old religious dispensation represented by the temple; the good wine is saved for last (2:10).

In chapters 3 and 4 Jesus encounters representatives of Jewish orthodoxy and heterodoxy in Nicodemus and the Samaritan woman respectively. Nicodemus, a Pharisee and ruler of the Jews, shows himself incapable of understanding and accepting God's new revelation in Jesus. He misunderstands Jesus repeatedly, because he takes his words in a commonplace, ordinary sense, whereas they are properly understood only with reference to Jesus and his revelation. "Rebirth" (or better "birth from above"; the Greek word is probably deliberately ambiguous) is the regeneration which occurs through faith in Jesus. Similarly, in the conversation with the woman of Samaria, the "living water" of which Jesus speaks is not "running water" (again probably a deliberate ambiguity in the Greek), but the water of eternal life which only Jesus can give. More than Nicodemus she is able to comprehend Jesus' words, and the result of her conversation with Jesus is the conversion of a number of her compatriots (4:39–42). While Nicodemus' meeting with Jesus had no positive outcome, Nicodemus himself reappears later on in the Gospel to defend Jesus (7:50–52) and assist at his burial (19:39). The judgment on him, whoever he may be, is not finally or unambiguously negative.

The original relationship of chapters 5 and 6 continues to be disputed among Johannine exegetes. Although something can be said for a rearrangement which puts chapter 6 before, instead of after, chapter 5 (thus allowing Jesus to remain in Galilee without a sudden removal to Jerusalem and return), the present order is not without apparent sense and purpose and is attested in all ancient manuscripts. After the miracle of the healing of the ruler's son (4:46–54), Jesus goes to Jerusalem for a feast (5:1). There he heals the crippled man at the pool of Bethzatha on the Sabbath, and, as a result, the Jews persecute him for breaking the law. Jesus then affirms his own filial relation to God (5:19ff.) and his oneness with him, especially in his life-giving work. Although Jesus is engaged for the most part in a monologue, his words have an argumentative tone, as though they are really intended to meet certain questions or objections. These may be adumbrated in 5:18, where the accusation that Jesus makes himself equal to God is recorded. At this point the tension between Jesus and his Jewish opposition reaches a new high. But it is then momentarily relieved by a sudden (and unexplained) return to Galilee (6:1), where Jesus feeds the five thousand (6:1–14). After he stills a storm at sea (vv. 16–21), there follows a long discourse and debate with those who have been fed (6:25–59) over the meaning of a scriptural passage—its exact OT source is uncertain—cited in 6:31: "He gave them bread from heaven to eat." Who or what is this bread? Is it the wilderness manna of the exodus or Jesus? Jesus' exposition of this passage, particularly his claim to be the bread from heaven, encounters astonishment and, again, misunderstanding among Jesus' interlocutors. Not only is the tension between Jesus and the Jews resumed, but even his disciples are perplexed and put off (6:60–65). Of course, Jesus does not mean that he is literally bread from heaven, but that he is the sustenance, the very stuff of the life which God gives. Quite possibly we should see in the talk about eating Jesus' flesh and drinking his blood (6:52–59) a scarcely veiled reference to the Christian eucharist. (Interestingly enough, there is no account of the institution of the Lord's Supper in John). The encounter with his disciples ends with what can only be considered a Johannine version of the confession of Peter (6:66–71), different in specific details as it may be.

In chapter 7 Jesus appears once again in Jerusalem, after a curious scene in which he first rebuffs the suggestion of his brothers that he go and then without explanation reverses himself (7:1–10). Very quickly conflict once again develops and Jesus' opponents, now identified as the chief priests and Pharisees, send officers to arrest him. The latter, however, are impressed by Jesus and at the end of chapter 7 refuse to do so, much to the chagrin of the Pharisees. The beginning of chapter 8 does not fit smoothly with what precedes. Jesus simply begins to speak at 8:12 without any reference to what has gone before, or to any setting at all. (The story of the woman taken in adultery, 7:53—8:11, was doubtless inserted at this point in many manuscripts because of the seeming lacuna, although it is certainly not a part of the original Gospel.) The Pharisees are, nevertheless, on hand and a heated argument follows in which the most serious accusations are exchanged.

With chapters 5 and 6, chapters 7 and 8 form a crucial central segment of the Gospel, in which the animosity of Jesus' opponents, called simply the Jews or else specified as Pharisees, is manifest and their lethal intent becomes clear. After this scene there is scarcely a suggestion of any rapprochement between them, with the possible exception of the role played by Nicodemus (7:50–52; 19:39). This central section is roughly comparable to the two cycles of feeding stories followed by the confession of Peter (8:27ff.) and the passion predictions in Mark's Gospel. In fact, John 6 like Mark 6—8 contains a feeding story, an adventure at sea, and a confession of Peter.

In chapter 9 the hostility of Jewish leaders is portrayed in narrative form, as they refuse to draw the proper inferences from Jesus' restoration of sight to the blind man (see below, chap. 4). Chapter 10, in which Jesus speaks of himself as the good shepherd, again eventuates in a heated controversy. The raising of Lazarus, God's restoration of life through Jesus (chap. 11), leads to a firm decision for Jesus' death on the part of his opponents (11:45–53). After a brief withdrawal from public view (11:54), Jesus once again goes to Jerusalem (chap. 12), enters the city triumphantly (12:12–19), and makes a series of pronouncements, his last public utterances before his death. The appearance of some Greeks seeking Jesus (12:20) doubtless prefigures the spread of the good news about him beyond Judaism, and his Jewish enemies, to the Greco-Roman world.

The Ministry to His Disciples

From chapters 13 through 17 Jesus is alone with his disciples (a group presumably, but not expressly, limited to the twelve). Chapters 18—19 narrate the crucifixion, chapter 20 (and 21) the resurrection. Chapter 13 contains the famous scene in which Jesus washes the feet of his disciples. Chapters 14 through 16 consist of the farewell discourses; Jesus gives his disciples words of consolation and encouragement. In chapter 17 he prays for them. The passion narrative (chaps. 18—19) begins with the arrest of Jesus (18:1–11), centers upon the long trial before Pilate (18:28—19:16), and, like the synoptic account, concludes with the story of Jesus' burial (19:38–42). The resurrection stories begin, as in the synoptics, with an account of the discovery of the empty tomb (20:1–10), which is followed by a series of appearance stories, unique to John, culminating in the renowned "doubting Thomas" scene with which the Gospel was originally intended to conclude.

The Johannine feet washing (13:1–11) occurs at the Last Supper and stands in lieu of the synoptic (and Pauline) tradition of the institution of the Lord's Supper. The Jesus of John's Gospel nowhere commands or institutes this

Christian sacrament. Following the washing of the feet there is an interpreta-tion of the deed (13:12–17),[15] after which the story of the identification of Judas as the betrayer, an event also found in the synoptic tradition (Mark 14:17–21), appears. There follows a brief series of sayings of Jesus, concluding with the love commandment (13:31–35). Peter's denial is then foretold (13:36–38; cf. Mark 14:26–31).

At 14:1 the farewell discourses proper begin, although the setting and the personae remain the same. They are a distant Johannine cousin of the eschato-logical discourses of the synoptics (Mark 13 parr.), dealing from a Johannine perspective with some of the same issues, i.e., the return of Jesus (see below) and the conduct (and welfare) of the disciples in this world. An anomaly occurs in 14:25–31, esp. vv. 30–31, where Jesus seems to conclude the dis-course in the expectation of his imminent arrest ("Rise, let us go hence"). Yet the discourses do not end, but prove to be at most only a third finished. Quite possibly chapters 15—16 (17) represent an alternative version of chapter 14, or a later appendage, or both.[16] In any event, the discourses have another formal ending in 16:29–33. But Jesus does not yet go to the cross which awaits him. First, he prays at length for the disciples (chap. 17); only afterward does the passion account proper begin.

In organization and content the Johannine passion narrative has the most extensive and closest parallels with the synoptics. With the exception of Jesus' conversation with Pilate and occasional Johannine touches (e.g., 18:6, 9; 19:30), it is in its general character and outlook not dissimilar to the synoptics, despite numerous differences of detail. The same may be said of the narrative of the discovery of the empty tomb (20:1–10; perhaps even vv. 11–18), as also of the resurrection appearance by the sea (21:1–14). But the appearances to the disciples behind closed doors (20:19–29) and the risen Jesus' conversation with Peter (21:15–24) are marked by numerous Johannine themes.

The whole of chapter 21 presents something of a structural anomaly, since the Gospel seems to conclude at 20:30–31. Probably at one time it did end, or was intended to end, at that point. But chapter 21 was surely added at an early date, if it is an appendage, for no manuscripts of the Gospel without that chapter have survived. In this appendix, 21:25 seems to be modeled on 20:30–31 and was probably written with that concluding colophon in view. If chapter 21 was added to the Gospel after it was deemed complete, it does not necessarily follow that all the material or tradition of that chapter is secondary to, or later than, chapter 20 or the remainder of the Gospel. Despite 21:14, 21:1–13 is apparently the account of an *initial* resurrection appearance at which the disciples are appropriately surprised and amazed. Somewhat analogous to this double ending of John's Gospel is the double ending of the farewell dis-courses, to which we have already referred. Quite possibly in both cases more than one Johannine tradition or narrative existed and both were incorporated, despite the resulting anomaly, into the final recension of the Gospel. Yet the fact that chapter 21 speaks to some problems of the subsequent generation which the Gospel as it stands leaves unresolved (e.g., the final status of Peter, the death of the Beloved Disciple and the delay of the parousia, the apostolic authority behind the Gospel, the relation of Peter to the Beloved Disciple) bespeaks the secondary character of the chapter in its present form.

We have seen that the second half of the Fourth Gospel consists of two or three major divisions, the farewell discourses and the passion and resurrection narratives. The discourses break down into the opening scene at the Last Supper (chap. 13), the prayer of Jesus (chap. 17), and the two recensions of the discourses proper (chap. 14; chaps. 15—16). The passion narrative, although consisting of individual units, is a continuous narrative. The resurrection narrative, of which there are again two recensions (chaps. 20 and 21), consists, as in the synoptics, of a story of the discovery of the empty tomb and various narratives of appearances of Jesus.

Despite the division between the public ministry and the ministry to his disciples which occurs at the end of chapter 12, the Gospel of John manifests an overall unity of style, theme, and content that distinguishes it among the Gospels. It portrays Jesus Christ as the only Son of God, who knows where he has come from and where he is going, that is, that he has come from God, and through his acceptance of the cross goes to God. The truth of Jesus' origin is spelled out in the prologue, referred to again in the discourses (16:28) and Jesus' prayer (17:5, 24), and, indeed, at other points in the Gospel (e.g., 6:38). The end and goal of Jesus' ministry, his return through the crucifixion to his original glory, is a recurring theme of the Gospel (12:23-24; 14:1-3; 17:1-5, 13, 23; 20:17).

The startling claims made for and by Jesus in the Gospel must elicit a sharp and decisive reaction. Those who oppose Jesus do not know the truth of his origin and goal and therefore regard his claims as presumption and blasphemy. They represent the world that is hostile to and condemned by God. On the other hand, the disciples, those who believe the Christian claims for Jesus (which in John are uttered by Jesus himself), are joined to him, sustained by him, and unified with him in this life and hereafter. While the destiny of the world is death, the destiny of Jesus' own is eternal life. This sharp dualism is embodied in the structure of John's Gospel. In the first half of the Gospel (chaps. 2—12) Jesus presents himself before a world that judges and rejects him, finally condemning him to death. Although the death does not occur until later, at the end of chapter 12 there is no doubt about its inevitability. The judgment of this world is not, however, the last word. Ultimately, it is to be overruled (12:31-32); but before that has become evident, a small group of believers, those whom God has given to Jesus, come out of the world to cast their lot with him. The last half of the Gospel (chaps. 13—20, 21) portrays Jesus with his own, instructing them, comforting them, and preparing them to continue in this world even though they do not belong to it. The sure ground of their life in Christ is not destroyed when the world does its worst to him; its reality is confirmed in his resurrection.

EXEGESIS

Exegesis is the explanation or elucidation of texts. The term is based on a Greek verb, *exegeomai,* which means to "lead forth" or "narrate." The exegesis of a text is then the leading forth of its meaning. In Part II we turn to specific Johannine texts, four from the Gospel and one from the letters, in order to lead forth their meaning.

Our working assumption is that these texts were written by a Christian author or authors in order to communicate the Christian message or some aspect of it. The exegesis will be a leading forth in the sense of a narration in that we shall read through these texts, commenting on their distinctive, significant and problematic features. The leading question will be, What did the ancient author intend to say to his readers? In some respects we may find it difficult, or even impossible, to answer this question with certainty. The texts may suggest things to us that the author never intended to say. Such suggestions may be significant and valuable. Nevertheless, we shall continue to pursue the question of what the texts as they have been composed would have meant to their first readers. From there we are one step away from understanding what the author (or authors) intended to convey. After examining these Johannine texts we shall turn to various significant historical, literary, and theological matters and issues which affect the problem of interpretation (Part III).

The first text, the prologue, embodies what we might call the cosmic perspective of the Fourth Gospel. The Word incarnate in Jesus Christ is set in the context of the creation. The next two texts represent a historical perspective in two senses: on the face of it they describe actions (miracles) and discourses of Jesus, a historical figure; but there is reason to think that they also reflect the historical circumstances of the Christian community from which the Gospel sprang. The final pair of texts are drawn from the farewell discourses of the Gospel and from 1 John. They both represent a present stage in the life of the church, that is, the ancient Johannine church. In the one case Jesus is speaking, but he speaks to his disciples, who are representative of the Christian community that arises out of his earthly ministry. Even though the disciples may not yet be able to understand (16:31–32), Jesus speaks of matters they will be able to understand after he has departed (16:4). In the passage from 1 John not Jesus but the author, who obviously bears authority derived from Jesus, speaks directly to the church, or to those communities for which he feels responsibility. Exegetes have recently argued that parts of the farewell discourses reflect the same situation, or address the same issues, as the Epistles. Whether this is the case is debatable, but we may bear this question in mind as we examine these texts.

CHAPTER THREE

THE JOHANNINE PERSPECTIVE: THE COSMIC, ETERNAL DIMENSION (1:1–18)

The language and style of the prologue (1:1–18) of John's Gospel is not entirely typical of the book as a whole. For one thing, the Gospel portrays Jesus as acting or talking; it is narrative and discourse. The prologue, however, speaks in the third person of his pre-existence, his relation to God and to creation. Moreover, not until the end of the prologue is the name of Jesus Christ called (1:17). Throughout the prologue he is described principally as the Word (*logos*), but also as the light (*phos*). Although in the Gospel proper Jesus occasionally refers to himself as the light (e.g., 8:12; 9:5), he is never, after the prologue, called the Word or *logos*. The Gospel is filled with numerous links or allusions to the historical circumstances of its origin, but these are not obvious in the prologue. Nevertheless, the prologue's perspective really agrees with that of the rest of the Gospel, and this is confirmed by how well it prepares the reader for what follows. The prologue may not be the best possible introduction to the historical circumstances under which the Gospel was written, but it is what the author of the Gospel intended that his reader should read first. What it says and suggests about Jesus provides the necessary introduction for appreciating the role that he plays in the Gospel. In the prologue Jesus Christ is set within a cosmic frame. He is portrayed as eternal, pre-existent, the agent of creation.

In the synoptic Gospels, especially Mark, the question of who Jesus is looms importantly in the background. In John that question becomes explicit and never lacks for an answer. Who is Jesus? At the very outset he is declared to be the Word of God, with the Father from the beginning, present and active in creation, etc. The answer is, in fact, given before the question can be raised. Or, to put it another way, John says, "There is the Word who was with God from the beginning, who was God's instrument in creation, who may himself be called God." It is as if these realities are known, or regarded as given, by the author and his readers. Then he asks, "Where or who is he?" The answer to that question is found in the entire Gospel, but it is already clearly indicated in the prologue: "The Word became flesh and dwelt among us . . ." (1:14); ". . . Grace and truth came through Jesus Christ" (1:17). The Gospel then becomes, and is rightly read as, the filling out in narrative form of a distinct understanding of who this Jesus is.

The style of the prologue is not unlike the rest of the Gospel, although noth-

ing exactly like it occurs again. Its rhythmic, poetic character can best be perceived in Greek, especially when the text is printed in strophic form. But even
the English translation conveys something of its solemn and portentous
character. A peculiar chain-like progression results from the repetition of key
words in verses 1–5:

> In the beginning was the *Word;*
> the *Word* was in God's presence,
> and the Word was *God.*
> He was present with God in the beginning.
> Through him all things *came into being,*
> and apart from him not a thing *came to be.*
> That which had *come to be* in him was *life,*
> and this *life* was the *light* of men.
> The *light* shines on in the *darkness,*
> for the *darkness* did not overcome it.[17]

Although the sequence of repetition is not perfect, it is nevertheless pronounced and distinctive. The poetic structure of the prologue is sharply
broken by prose passages in 1:6–8 and 15, which refer not to the Word or light,
the subject of the rest of the prologue, but to John the Baptist. In addition,
several other verses (e.g., 13) may fall outside the basic poetic structure.

Quite possibly we have here an early Christian hymn that the author has
annotated and incorporated into his Gospel. (Cf. Phil. 2:6–11; Col. 1:15–20;
and 1 Tim. 3:16 for other such hymns.) The hymn may even be pre-Christian
in origin, but if so the Evangelist probably adopted and adapted it from his
own church. When the possible redactional additions and annotations are
stripped away, its language, style, and theology are still "Johannine"; the basic
hymn and the Gospel appear to share a common perspective and vocabulary.

The RSV paragraphing offers an initial clue to the character and content of
the prologue: vv. 1–5 are a literary unit, the first part of the prologue poem
or hymn; vv. 6–8, a prosaic interruption; the second section of the hymn, vv.
9–12 (13), is followed by another and concluding section, vv. 14–18 (less v. 15,
another prosaic redactional addition). These divisions correspond roughly to
the thematic divisions of the prologue. In vv. 1–5 the theme is God, creation,
and the Word; in vv. 6–8, John the Baptist; in vv. 9–13, the Word in the world;
and in vv. 14–18, the community's confession of the Word.

We must now ask in greater detail: What is the meaning of the prologue?
What is its relation to the rest of the Gospel? An answer to these questions
must proceed by way of an analysis of the key term Word (Greek, *logos*). Who
or what is the Word? In the first place, the Word is Jesus Christ (cf. v. 17).
But in vv. 1–5 does the author intend to speak of the man Jesus of Nazareth,
of the pre-existent Christ, or of a Christ principle? He can hardly mean that
Jesus of Nazareth was with God before all creation and that he was the mediator of all creation. Where, moreover, does this concept of the Word originate?

It is perhaps to be understood against the background of Greek philosophy, in which the term and concept of *logos* were quite important. Or it may be seen against the background of the OT and Jewish concept of the word of the Lord. It is clear that in the Gospel and in the prologue the Word *denotes* Jesus Christ; what more it *connotes* remains to be determined.

The Greek philosophical meanings of *logos* are probably only remotely related to John's use of the term. The Stoic understanding of *logos* as the world principle is not to be translated into the Word which is Jesus Christ. Nevertheless, we cannot ignore the broad range of meanings of the Greek term *logos*: explanation, argument, principle, thought or reason, language, speech, and divine utterance. Any of these may be relevant for understanding John. So too the use of the term in late Jewish and pagan religious texts to designate God's agent in creation and in world government is significant. Such a usage occurs particularly in Hellenistic Jewish texts where word is sometimes identified with wisdom (Greek, *sophia*) and understood as God's means of communication with the world. It is clear enough that the *logos* of John is God's speech, his self-disclosure to the world, and, as the text makes plain, the means through which God creates. This range of meaning is quite intelligible against the background of contemporary usage.

The OT and Jewish conceptions of the word of God also hover in the background. Doubtless John would have agreed that the word of God which spoke through the prophets was now incarnate in Jesus Christ. Nothing in the text, however, indicates that precisely this thought was at the center of his attention when he wrote. The most obvious and immediate background of the concept of the Word is the Genesis creation story, which also opens with "in the beginning." Moreover, John like Genesis intends to speak of the creation. Although there is no statement in Genesis that God created all things by the Word, each stage of creation is portrayed as resulting from God's speaking: "And God said, 'Let there be light'; and there was light" (Gen. 1:3). In Genesis God first creates light, and John initially (1:5, 7–9) describes Jesus' appearance in the world in terms of light. Moreover, the motifs of darkness and light appear over against one another in both. In Genesis God speaks and there is light where darkness had heretofore prevailed; God then separates the light from the darkness (1:3–5), and there is night and day. In John's prologue, the contrast between light and darkness is developed in the direction of a sharply defined dualism, which is characteristic of the Gospel as a whole. The similarity between John and Genesis reveals a common ground on which they stand. But the striking dualism of John shows that the Gospel, unlike Genesis, belongs in the first-century religious world. Such fundamental distinctions between light and darkness, truth and falsehood, God and Satan, and so on, were common not only to Zoroastrianism, Gnosticism, and late Platonism, but also to certain forms of Judaism antecedent to and contemporary with the Fourth Gospel. That such a world view could arise within the bounds of first-century

Palestinian Judaism has been evidenced by the discovery of the Qumran scrolls, in which we find a dualistic view of the world, men, and events very similar to that of the Gospel of John.

It would be misleading to suggest, however, that to understand the prologue one must first understand the Greek use of *logos,* the OT creation story, and various aspects of first-century sectarian Judaism. Investigation of all such contexts is helpful, but John speaks intelligibly apart from them, even though he can be fully understood only within them. Perhaps this is why John has always been a popular Gospel among Christians, most of whom have not had an accurate conception of its historical background. Probably the basis of John's intelligibility for Christians is that he intends to speak only about Jesus Christ. His choice of terminology and the use of motifs from the Genesis creation story turn upon his purpose of setting forth the meaning and significance of Jesus. This holds true even though the name Jesus does not occur until the end (v. 17). A Christian reader would know that the Word was Jesus Christ before he read further in the Gospel, although the name of Jesus is not called until the prologue has moved from the cosmic or the metaphysical plane to the historical. He would thus be able to understand the prologue on the basis of common Christian tradition. Whatever audience the author intended, most of the Gospel's readers are and have been Christian.

The movement from the rather abstract, if dramatic and impressive, talk about the *logos* to the level of historical events takes place by stages. Verses 1 and 2 deal with the relation of the Word to God, which is defined in the closest possible terms without John's saying that *logos* and God are simply equivalent. The statement, "And the Word was God," is immediately qualified by "He was in the beginning with God." In addition, the Greek of the former statement lacks the definite article (*ho* = "the") before "God," which in Greek indicates something less than a total identification of the word with God.[18] Nevertheless, in vv. 3 and 4 the most exalted status and functions are attributed to the Word.

Did the Evangelist actually think that the man Jesus created the world? He does not say exactly this. But clearly he thinks of the pre-existence of Jesus, not merely of the Word of God (cf. 17:5). We cannot deny that he could have entertained this idea. The interpreter must remember, however, that this is a line from a poem or hymn, not a piece of philosophical or theological prose. (The statement of 17:5 occurs in the context of a prayer, whose formulation may have been influenced by the way early Christians actually worshiped and prayed.) The early prayers, hymns, and similar formulations of the NT frequently speak of the pre-existent Christ (cf. Phil. 2:6–7 and Col. 1:15–16, for example); in 1 Cor. 8:6 Paul, in a liturgical or semi-liturgical formula, refers to "one Lord, Jesus Christ, through whom are all things and through whom we exist," as if Jesus Christ were God's instrument in creation (cf. also Heb. 1:2–3). So the idea of Christ playing a role in creation is not distinctively

Johannine, but is characteristic of early Christian faith. Moreover, such affirmations tend to occur in solemn, liturgical, formulations, a fact which does not mean they were not seriously meant, but does caution against our understanding them prosaically or literally.

To most of us the idea that the *man* Jesus was the agent by whom God created the world is very strange. But for NT faith, and particularly for Johannine Christianity, Jesus Christ is not to be equated simply with the historical man Jesus of Nazareth, although he is inseparable from him. He is the Son of God, the Word of God, the Christ, the Son of man. In him God reveals himself to man and acts on behalf of man in a decisive way. The terms and categories that we find appropriate to describe historical persons and events can no longer quite comprehend him. In him the God who creates the world now saves it from its evil and folly. God's action in creation and redemption are one. Over against any purely otherworldly spirituality John affirms that the Word by which God creates the world is the same Word by which he redeems it. This Word can be identified with a special historical person and event, Jesus, whom John will name before the prologue is complete. To ask whether John, or any other NT writer, conceives of the man Jesus as working alongside God in creation is really to ask a question that leads away from, rather than toward, the essential theological point about the unity of creation, revelation, and redemption in Christ. The God who creates through his Word also reveals himself and saves through the same Word. In John's view, since the coming of Jesus Christ this Word cannot be conceived in abstraction from him.

Whether v. 5 refers to the Word present in creation at the beginning and throughout history or to the Word revealed in Jesus is a real question. As it stands the statement probably applies to the historic Jesus Christ, the Word become flesh.[19] Yet the prologue may be read down to v. 14 on the assumption that the author is speaking of God's activity through his Word first in creation (vv. 1–4) and then in revelation. In vv. 10–13, however, it becomes increasingly clear that the Evangelist must have Jesus Christ already in view, whether or not the non-Christian reader of the Gospel would have realized this. That the Evangelist had Jesus in view in v. 5 is supported by the presence of the passage dealing with the Baptist (vv. 6–8). The Baptist comes before Jesus, preparing his way. Thus, the first suggestion of Jesus' presence in the world, if that is to be found in v. 5, evokes the recollection of John the Baptist; and the mention of the Baptist leads in turn to the first explicit reference to Jesus' coming (vv. 9ff.).

John (vv. 6–8) is a man from God, a witness sent beforehand that all men, or at least all Israel, might believe. He is the forerunner. This role is already fixed by the earlier tradition. The Evangelist also has the Baptist deny that he is the light (v. 8), probably indicating that already in v. 5 he understands the light to be Jesus himself. This and subsequent negative statements about John the Baptist, in which he typically denies he is the Christ, may represent a subtle polemic against certain of his disciples. Disciples of the Baptist are mentioned in the Gospels and Acts (18:25), but John's Gospel affords the most tangible evidence that there was an actual rivalry between the early church and the Baptist sect, possibly extending back all the way to the period of Jesus' ministry.[20] In any event, the Evangelist wishes to emphasize the singular importance of Jesus by asserting his superiority to any rival, particularly John. The witness of John the Baptist appears again in v. 15 (cf. v. 30), and somewhat awkwardly, indicating that v. 15, like vv. 6–8, is probably an interpolation. Again we observe a polemical interest; John bears witness as much against himself as for Jesus.

The prologue moves back to a poetic style (v. 9) and to the themes of the first five verses, as John thinks of the coming of Jesus Christ into the world (vv. 9–13). The "world" is used in two different senses (v. 10)—creation ("the world was made through him") and the world of men ("the world knew him not"). The second usage is characteristic of the Fourth Gospel and 1 John; it implies the world in alienation from God. "His own people" (v. 11) may be mankind generally or Israel, the Jews, probably the latter. Their rejection of Jesus is portrayed in the first half of the Gospel (chaps. 2—12), and is made especially explicit in the closing verses of chapter 12. By rejecting Jesus, the Jews become the prime representatives of the world in the negative sense. In the last half of the Gospel (chaps. 13—20) this world, whether Jew or Gentile, forms the hostile background against which Jesus gathers together his community of disciples, the church. Although "the world" sums up man's opposition to Jesus in John, there is another sense in which the world is the object of God's love. He sends Jesus, who saves the world (3:16) while overcoming it (16:33).

Having indicated the rejection of Jesus, the Evangelist now speaks of those who receive him, that is, "believe in his name." As in the OT "name" indicates more than just the verbal designation of a person. It signifies the reality and importance of the person himself. To believe in Jesus' name is not merely to confess him verbally, but to have faith in who and what he is. To all who so believe, Jesus gives power or authority to become children of God, who are born through no human agency, but through the will of God (see John 3). In John those who are begotten by God are, of course, begotten by faith.

In 1:14 John for the first time speaks directly of Jesus' historical and human presence. This verse is often cited as the primary scriptural basis for belief in the incarnation, the Christian doctrine that in Jesus God became man. It has served as a bulwark against any Gnostic or docetic watering down of the full humanity of the Word. In contrast to a modern state of mind that looks with skepticism upon any claims of manifestations of God in human life and history, ancient man was, by and large, willing and able to entertain a variety of such claims. Thus the idea that God had in some form dwelt among men was not so likely to give offense as the claim that the one who fully reveals God is nevertheless a man whose origins can on one level be accounted for quite naturally (cf. 1:45–46; 7:15, 41, 52; 8:58). This paradox is a constant source of consternation and offense throughout the first half of the Fourth Gospel. John's statement that the Word became flesh is unique in the NT. Nevertheless, it does not stand out as a strange or foreign body. If anything, the reverse is true; it has been taken to be a kind of summation of the NT view of Christ, and in a real sense it is. The interpretation of the meaning and significance of Jesus as presented in the whole range of NT teaching is aptly epitomized in John's statement that the Word became flesh.

The Word not only became flesh or man, Jesus as a man was "full of grace and truth." Here a Pauline and early Christian term, *grace,* is combined with the distinctively Johannine *truth.* By the time John wrote, *grace* was probably a part of the standard Christian vocabulary, a brief but meaningful way of referring to all God had done in Jesus. Although the word *truth* was certainly not strange to Christian ears, John is noteworthy for the way in which he applies the term to Jesus himself. "I am the way, the truth, and the life," says Jesus to Thomas and the other disciples in the farewell discourses (14:6). Jesus is truth. This statement does not mean he is the right in contrast to the wrong, or the correct in contrast to the erroneous, not even the true in contrast to the false in the usual sense. He is the real, the embodiment of the reality of God in contrast to everybody and everything that is false and deceptive.[21] In short, he is the one upon whom one can depend, and who will not fail, in contrast to all the false supports and securities of life.

Concentration upon the doctrine of the incarnation has, however, probably meant that the rest of this verse (14) has not received the attention it deserves. The fact of Jesus Christ's coming is not introduced but made explicit or summarized in the statement that the Word became flesh. Although its significance as a concise summation of Christian belief is undeniable, the latter half of the verse is also important in the development of the Gospel. Not only has this extraordinary, gracious, and true man dwelt among men, but at least some of them have seen him for who he is. Thus, "*We* have beheld his glory. . . ." (Note the change to the first person plural, signifying the witnessing and believing community.) His glory is the presence and activity of God in him. In OT and Jewish thought *glory* is the shining radiance of God's presence, thought to have dwelt in the temple. The verb *dwell* in this same verse may also have the more specific meaning of "to pitch a tent," "to tabernacle." According to Jewish tradition God dwelt in his temple as in a tabernacle or tent. Indeed, according to the OT, the ancient predecessor of the Jerusalem temple was a tabernacle or tent, and God's glory, name, or presence dwelt there. Thus the dwelling of the Word among the people and the beholding of the glory are ideas with a prior relationship in Jewish thought. Against this background the thrust of the Evangelist's statements becomes even clearer.

Jesus is the new temple or tabernacle, the new place where God manifests himself to man, where his glory is beheld (cf. 2:19-22). The description of this glory, "as of the only Son from the Father," is typically Johannine. In John, Jesus is the Son and God is his Father in a special sense.

The first half of the Gospel (chaps. 2—12) provides a partial answer to the question of how and when the divine glory appears. It is manifest in the word and especially the deeds of Jesus, called signs. As we have noted, the use of miracles as signs of Jesus' glory in John sets the Gospel in sharp contrast to the synoptics, where Jesus refuses to do miracles as signs in this sense. Yet Jesus' glory is not simply his miraculous power. The supreme manifestation of the glory is his death on the cross (cf. especially 12:23ff.).

When John writes, "We have beheld his glory," he perhaps means or includes the apostolic *we* (cf. 1 John 1:1ff.). Certainly the authoritative witness in the church attests the glory of Christ. The "we have beheld" is founded upon the apostolic eyewitness of Jesus Christ, but is not limited to it. Physical seeing of Jesus is not disparaged by the author. In fact, it is a necessity, but in and of itself it may be of no particular advantage. Faith has direct access to Jesus. At the end of the Gospel, Jesus says to "doubting Thomas," who has just received physical evidence of the resurrection, "Have you believed because you have seen me? Blessed are those who have not seen and yet believe" (20:29). Moreover, genuine seeing is not confined to physical sight, but involves true perception of the nature of a person or thing (cf. chaps. 9 and 14). "We have beheld his glory," therefore, does not simply vouch for the apostolicity or authenticity of an eyewitness standing behind the Gospel. The "we" who speak are not necessarily first-generation Christians or the disciples of the historical Jesus, but all those who have rightly perceived the Word of God in Jesus Christ and have thereby beheld his glory.

After the second reference to the Baptist (v. 15), the theme of the incarnate glory is again taken up (v. 16). The fact that here the *we* so obviously means the Christian community supports our contention that the whole church is included in the *we* of v. 14. The fullness (v. 16) is presumably the fullness of grace and truth in the Word become flesh (v. 14), as is confirmed by the concluding phrase "grace upon grace" which probably ought to be understood in the sense of "grace abounding." Jesus and Moses are then set over against one another in almost Pauline fashion, with Moses representing the law and grace and truth again associated with Jesus Christ (v. 17). Only now is Jesus actually named, and his identity with the Word put beyond question. In a skillful way the prologue leads the reader up to the point at which Jesus' name is called. A certain dramatic sense, demonstrated throughout the Gospel, appears at the outset as the Evangelist builds toward the climax of the prologue. Although the polarity between Moses as lawgiver and Jesus as the source of grace and truth occupies an important place in the prologue, it is not prominent in the rest of the Gospel. The central problem for Paul, the relation of law and grace, has apparently become for John a thing of the past. Later he calls the Jewish law "your law," clearly indicating that the law as such is now considered only an aspect or institution of the Jewish religion (8:17). Yet there is in the Fourth Gospel a recurring juxtaposition of Jesus and Moses, in which Jesus emerges as the superior.[22]

The concluding verse (18) presents a textual problem; all the ancient manuscripts do not agree. Probably the reading *God* (RSV, footnote) is to be preferred over *Son,* even though *only Son* accords somewhat better with John's usage elsewhere.[23] If so, then we should have to read "only begotten God," or the like. Jesus as only begotten God would not, however, be a concept incompatible to John, particularly in view of his understanding of him as the creating and revealing Word. The point is clear enough. That no one had ever seen God would have been a commonplace to the educated Jew or the sophisticated Greek, although some contemporary Jewish mystical thought may have been concerned with the question of whether Moses had seen God. Be that as it may, the author's intention is to point once again to the definitive character of the revelation of God in Christ: "he has made him known." In a real sense, v. 18 reiterates the message of vv. 14–17. The glory of God is manifest for the salvation of man in Jesus.

As v. 14 points forward to the revelation of the glory in Jesus' public ministry culminating in his death, vv. 16–18 point to the revelation of the glory of God in a fuller, more immediate way to the Christian church, the community of Jesus' disciples. If the end of Jesus' public ministry seems outwardly to be his rejection (12:37–43) and death, that end, in light of his more intimate concluding revelations to his disciples, is really their believing, seeing, and knowing (chap. 16). Yet, as we shall see, John knows that this fuller knowledge did not actually occur during Jesus' earthly life. After the resurrection, when the Spirit has come and the church is properly founded, the meaning and significance of his life and death is to be more fully understood and appreciated by his own followers. Thus the prologue leaves the reader anticipating the ministry of Jesus, its conflict and his rejection and death. There is also ample indication that this rejection is not the last word. In the world's eyes, or on any purely empirical basis, it might have seemed to be the final and definitive judgment against Jesus. Yet the realities that the world knows do not govern Jesus, who marches to another drumbeat. The reality that determines and governs him is suggested by the cosmic and theological language of the prologue. Jesus antedates and is superior to the men, institutions, and forces of darkness which would do him in. Despite the opposition and rejection that the Gospel reports, the ultimate origin and the destiny of Jesus are grounded in his relationship to God and in God's eternal purpose for him. "In the beginning was the Word, and the Word was with God, and the Word was God."

CHAPTER FOUR

THE JOHANNINE PERSPECTIVE: THE PAST, HISTORICAL DIMENSION (CHAPTERS 5 AND 9)

The miracle stories of the Fourth Gospel are distinctive. They are significantly fewer than the synoptic stories, but if anything more important, for they are signs manifesting Jesus' glory. The sheerly miraculous element seems to be heightened in John, yet the acts themselves are no more sensational than in the other Gospels. After all, Jesus appears as a mighty miracle worker in Mark. By and large John develops each miracle story more fully by showing Jesus talking with bystanders and opponents about its significance. This Johannine emphasis upon the explanatory discourses of Jesus reflects his concentration on the miracles as "signs" (see 6:26ff. and cf. 20:30–31).

The Fourth Gospel also employs a somewhat different collection of miracle stories. The transformation of water into wine at Cana (2:1–12) has no parallel in the synoptics; nor do the stories of the Samaritan woman (chap. 4—Jesus' knowledge of her is miraculous), the man at the sheep gate pool (chap. 5), the man born blind (chap. 9), and the raising of Lazarus (chap. 11). Jesus' foreknowledge of Nathanael (1:45–51) may also be miraculous, in which case it also has no parallel. On the other hand, the bread miracle (6:1–14), the walking on the water (6:16–21), and the healing of the ruler's son (4:46–54) have definite synoptic parallels (cf. Mark 6:32–44; 6:45–51; and Matt. 8:5–10, respectively). Some events or incidents—including the passion narrative—have clear synoptic parallels but are not miraculous (cf. 2:13–22; 12:1–11; 12:12–19; 13:21–30). Of the miracle stories found only in John, those of chapters 5 and 9 are similar to several synoptic stories. The changing of water into wine, however, is a feat unparalleled in the synoptics, where Jesus' miracles are characteristically healings or demon exorcisms. The latter are, of course, entirely lacking in John. Although Jesus raises the dead in the synoptics, there is nothing like the elaborate story of the raising of Lazarus anywhere else in the NT.

Some significance attaches to the arrangement of the miracle stories in John; most are especially suited for their positions in the Gospel. The miracle of the new wine symbolically introduces Jesus' public ministry. The story of Jesus' revelation to the Samaritan woman (chap. 4) stands directly over against the inability of Nicodemus, the teacher of Israel, to grasp his meaning (chap. 3). The miracles of chapters 5 and 6 are integrally related to the long dialogues which follow them. The most artfully constructed and theologically pregnant of the miracle stories (chaps. 9 and 11) appear last. In the one, Jesus restores the gift of sight (light), and in the other, life. The raising of Lazarus from the dead (chap. 11) gives concreteness to Jesus' claim that "as the Father raises the dead and gives them life, so also the Son gives life to whom he will" (5:21). The miracle graphically portrays the character of his mission and work, and leads directly to Jesus' own death, which, paradoxically, is the source of life to all who believe.

Despite the many distinctive characteristics of the Johannine miracles in comparison to the synoptic (especially the Markan), there are some remarkable points of contact or similarity, especially between John and Mark. In both Gospels the principal public activities of Jesus seem to be miracle working and teaching. While in Matthew and Luke Jesus' teaching is transmitted in some detail, in Mark it is rather sparsely represented, although Jesus is frequently described as teaching. In John Jesus' public discourses are actually more polemical than didactic, and he is not frequently represented as "teaching" (but see 7:14; 18:20). He even commands his disciples rather than teaching them. Nevertheless, he is called Rabbi or teacher (e.g., 1:28; 3:2), even in John, and the title is not misplaced.

The Johannine Jesus engages in frequent and lengthy discussions and debates with interlocutors and opponents. In fact, his miraculous deeds lead more than once to hostile encounters or reactions (chaps. 5, 7, 9, 11). There is an alternation between miraculous sign and controversy. Similarly, in Mark Jesus' miracles are sometimes portrayed as occurring in a hostile environment, and in fact elicit controversy (esp. in 2:1—3:6). Moreover, Jesus wages a recurrent struggle with demons as well as human opponents in Mark. In both Mark and John the reaction of the disciples to the miracles and controversy is as much perplexity as comprehension. Thus we have in John and Mark two rather different narratives with certain important elements in common: Jesus is a teacher, a miracle worker, and the object of hostility among his Jewish contemporaries, both for his teaching and for his miracles. Although Jesus abjures the quest for signs in Mark, as in the other synoptics, his miraculous deeds nevertheless seem to raise the question of who he is. John, although a very distinctive Gospel, nevertheless shares with Mark, and to a lesser degree with the other canonical Gospels, some basic notions of the character of the historic ministry of Jesus. From what little we know or can infer about Jesus from other, even non-Christian sources, these basic notions are not, historically speaking, misleading. Jesus actually taught, performed exorcisms and other healings regarded as marvelous, and became the object of hostility and controversy among his contemporaries. There is a historical element in the Johannine as well as the Markan (and synoptic) narrative of Jesus' public ministry that is authentic. There are also elements that reflect later historical situations and conflicts of the Johannine church. In this respect also John does not differ from the synoptics. In our exegesis we shall be interested in the peculiarly Johannine elements and the historical facts or situation they represent.

John 5

Both the similarities and the differences between John and the synoptic Gospels come to light in a remarkable way in John 5. In this chapter the characteristic themes of Johannine theology find expression. By examining it we shall be able to see how the Gospel of John qualifies as distinctly Christian preaching, in a way that even the synoptic Gospels do not.

The chapter begins rather abruptly. For good reason John has been called a seamless robe. The narrative moves with such clear intentionality, and often so smoothly, that the characterization seems apt. Yet at some points there are lacunae, breaks, abrupt stops and starts; and this is one of them. Jesus was last seen in Cana of Galilee; while there he healed the official's son, who lay at death's door in Capernaum. All of that, and whatever else may have been in the author's mind, seems to be summed up in the laconic "after this" of John 5:1. As the RSV renders it, "After this there was a feast of the Jews, and Jesus went up to Jerusalem." John then briefly recounts a miracle story in which Jesus heals a man whose illness is not clearly specified.

The story has some curious features. The name of the pool is not clear. The names Bethzatha, Bethesda, and Bethsaida appear in different manuscripts. The pool with its five porches may have been discovered by archaeologists. If so, the discovery perhaps illumines the historical background of the account more than John's purpose in recounting the story. Even before Jesus speaks to the man, he knows that he has been ill for a long time. When Jesus asks him whether he wishes to be well, he does not answer directly, but describes his problem in getting into the pool "when the water is troubled." Jesus pays as little attention to that response as the man apparently paid to Jesus' question. "Rise, take up your pallet, and walk," says Jesus. The word of Jesus exactly parallels Mark 2:9, where it occurs in quite a different healing narrative. Jesus may have said such a thing more than once, and it would be easily remembered. The man's remark about not being able to get down into the pool when the water was stirred up sounded so strange that some ancient copyist provided an explanation after John 5:3. (That is v. 4, relegated to a footnote in the RSV.)

Such difficulties as the story may present do not, however, prevent John's using it to portray Jesus and to say what in his view is crucially important about him. Probably the story was traditional, a story about Jesus' healing a person very much like many such stories that circulated among Christians and are found now in the Gospels. The oldest traditions about Jesus portray him as a miracle worker. Possibly its traditional character accounts in large part for the peculiarities of this story. Maybe the Evangelist himself did not know the name of the pool, exactly what illness affected the man, and so forth.

Nevertheless, the story also has a Johannine character, whether imposed by the Evangelist or already in the traditional story. Jesus knows, supernaturally and without asking, that the man has been lying ill for a long time. He does not wait to be approached (contrast John 4:47; Mark 2:2-4; 5:25-28; 7:25, 32; 8:22; 10:47), but initiates the healing. When the man responds to his question, Jesus takes no notice of it, but gives a command that effects the healing immediately and with no preparation. Such behavior is not uncharacteristic of the Jesus of the Fourth Gospel. He knows Nathanael before they meet; he also knows all about the Samaritan woman, who has never met him, and tells her about herself. Typically he initiates the conversation or action, and often seems not to notice what has been said to him but speaks at another level. This is characteristic. Jesus' interlocutors do not have the theological knowledge to comprehend what he means. By the same token, he utters statements that make little apparent contact with what has been said to him.

What we see so far is a miracle story that is not unlike a number of other miracles stories of the Gospel, except that it has certain Johannine features. John uses tradition and builds upon it in order to portray Jesus in a distinctive way, to make clear what to him is most important about Jesus. In the process it will become evident that the issues which move him and the situation he faces are different from those of Jesus' day. There is as yet no hint of the course the narrative will take. The man demonstrates that he has been healed by taking up his bed at Jesus' command—he walks. In a typical synoptic miracle story this would be the end of the account, or nearly so. We are still, however, near the beginning of this episode. We are now told that the healing had occurred on the Sabbath (John 5:9), a motif familiar from the synoptics. Jesus becomes involved in controversy because he violates, or to many seems to violate, the Sabbath. But in some contrast to the synoptics (e.g., Mark 3:1-6; cf. 2:23-28), the Sabbath motif has not figured prominently, or at all, in the story itself. Only now is it introduced. It is traditional at least in the sense that John gets it from tradition. He knows that Jesus was often accused of breaking the Sabbath.

But it is the healed man, not Jesus, who now is accused of breaking the Sabbath by carrying his pallet (John 5:10). (Similarly, in Mark 2:23-24, Jesus' disciples are attacked for plucking grain on the Sabbath.) The healed man responds by saying that Jesus has commanded him to do so (John 5:11). The Jews then ask him to identify the one who has commanded him. In the synoptic Gospels it is no mystery who works miracles and heals, although Jesus may command those healed to remain silent about his miracles. We also observe yet another striking feature. The people who challenge the healed man are described as Jews, which doubtless they were; but in this setting everyone, including Jesus, presumably would have been a Jew. All this is unusual, except in the Fourth Gospel, where it is characteristic.

Who is called a Jew, or when is a member of Israel called a Jew and by whom?[24] In the synoptic tradition it can be assumed that everyone is a Jew unless otherwise designated, so no one is ordinarily called that. Only when non-Jews appear is the term used. Thus the wise men from the East inquire about one born "king of the Jews" (Matt. 2:2), or Pilate designates Jesus "the King of the Jews" (Matt. 27:37 and parr.) after his Roman soldiers have mocked him. All this corresponds closely to first-century Palestinian Jewish usage. John's usage, on the other hand, does not conform to what we would expect from Jewish circles in first-century Palestine. The narrator somehow stands outside the orbit of Judaism in that he seems no longer to consider himself, or even Jesus and his disciples, to be Jewish. Of course, John can have Jesus addressed as a Jew by the Samaritan woman (John 4:9), and Jesus can even speak from the standpoint of Judaism (4:22). The Evangelist knows that Jesus is from Nazareth (1:45–46) of Galilee (7:41). Yet when Jesus or his retinue confronts hostile people in his homeland, the latter are characteristically and routinely referred to as "the Jews." Moreover, these Jews can distinguish between disciples of Jesus and disciples of Moses (John 9:28); one must choose between the two!

What we find in John is then a clear departure from synoptic usage. In the other Gospels Jesus may set himself off from Moses in an unprecedented way. He may call the Mosaic divorce law a concession because of "your hardness of heart" (Mark 10:5), and in the Sermon on the Mount may counterpose to Mosaic law his own, authoritative, "but I say to you," which characteristically radicalizes the Mosaic command. Yet all this stands in the context of Jew talking to Jew, and on the assumption that the (Jewish) scriptures contain the word of God, which Jews as such could understand, if only they would.

Jesus and his original disciples did not regard themselves as having abandoned Moses or Judaism, and the synoptic tradition reflects this state of affairs. When in a synoptic saying (Matt. 12:41–42; Luke 11:31–32) Jesus implies he is greater than Jonah or Solomon, he does not say he is greater than Moses. In John, however, Jesus says or implies that he is greater than Jacob (John 4:12–14), Abraham (John 8:56–58), and Moses (John 6:32–33, 49–51; cf. 5:45–47). In John Jesus presents a view of himself, a Christology, which he does not espouse in the other Gospels.

Both John and the synoptics were written in and for Christian communities. That is, they were written in and for Christian churches as distinguished from the synagogue. Yet in the synoptics the tradition still embodies, to a recognizable degree, a time and a perspective different from the authors' own—whether it be the perspective of Jesus or that of the post-resurrection Palestinian church, which lived in a Jewish environment where Aramaic was still spoken and people still looked for the coming redemption of Israel. (Cf. Luke 24:21 and Acts 1:6, which, although quite possibly compositions of Luke, are intended to convey the perspective of an earlier time.) John, on the other hand, reflects an entirely Christian point of view, and one in which it cannot be taken for granted that everyone involved in the drama is a Jew. Not only is this the Evangelist's perspective, but it permeates the material of which the Gospel is composed. And in this respect John differs significantly from the synoptics.

By commonly referring to Jesus' interlocutors as "the Jews," however, John creates the impression that Jesus does not belong, or no longer belongs, to the Jewish community. By the same token, neither do the disciples (John 9:28), nor does the Evangelist himself. Not only John, but Jesus also, speaks from the perspective of a community separate and distinct from Judaism. Jesus, as well as the Evangelist, talks like a Christian. (Yet the term "Christian" does not appear in the Gospel of John or in any of the Gospels.)

There follows upon the Jews' question to the healed man about the identity of his benefactor (v. 12) a rather strange interlude. Jesus is at first absent (v. 13), but then encounters the healed man in the temple and warns him (v. 14). The warning goes unheeded, for apparently the Evangelist would have us understand that the man betrayed Jesus to the Jews (v. 15)—that is, betrayed his identity—with the result that the Jews persecuted Jesus (v. 16). After the second encounter he knows, but curiously the text never says Jesus told him! There may well be an intentional contrast between this man, who instead of affirming or confessing Jesus betrays him, and the man born blind of chapter 9 (see below). The latter doggedly insists upon the reality of what Jesus has done for him in the face of severe questioning, even harassment, and finally confesses his faith in him (9:38). In any event, the fact of tension or opposition between Jesus and those who have been identified as "the Jews" is now established. They persecute him because of the healing he has performed on the Sabbath. At length Jesus speaks in response.

Jesus seems to speak in answer to no direct question but to the presumed situation as a whole. "My Father is working still, and I am working," he says (5:17). Jesus never justifies himself against the charge that he has broken the Sabbath with such an imperious statement in the synoptics, although he may imply that he is "Lord of the sabbath" (Mark 2:28). In the other Gospels he appeals to the precedent of David (Mark 2:24–26), to common sense (Mark 3:4), or to commonly accepted practice (Luke 13:15; 14:5). Here, in the Fourth Gospel, he compares his working on the Sabbath with God's working. If the other Gospels are our guide or criteria, it is unlikely that Jesus actually said this about himself. Rather, here the confessing community speaks. As the Johannine church believed that Jesus was in the beginning with God (John 1:1–2; 17:24) and at present with God in glory (17:24; 20:17, 26–29), so it also believed that as the Father always worked Jesus continued to work, whether during the week or on the Sabbath.

Jesus' response actually goes far beyond what is called for by the situation, injecting an entirely new and disturbing element into it, a view of himself that does not arise directly out of the situation or out of the healing narrative. It is a view well calculated to arouse the ire of anyone, particularly any Jew, who does not share the christological views of the Johannine community: "This was why the Jews sought all the more to kill him, because he not only broke the sabbath but also called God his own Father, making himself equal to God" (5:18). Moreover, the claim Jesus makes for himself, as well as the issue to which it speaks, is foreign to the synoptic tradition.

Significantly, the Jews' persecution of Jesus is suddenly presented as already in the progress, suddenly attaining its full intensity—they were seeking to kill Jesus—without its development having been described in narrative form. Intense opposition between Jesus and the Jews dominates the Fourth Gospel from this point. Heretofore, the reaction of the Jews (John 2:13-22) and of their representative Nicodemus (John 3:1-21), has been perplexity rather than hostility. The same is true of the Samaritan woman. Hereafter, although there may be moments of uncertainty, the Jews of the Fourth Gospel, including those who have believed in Jesus (John 8:31), are not only estranged from Jesus but for the most part hostile to him.

Now John not only preaches Jesus as the Christ of Christian confession but presents him in a decidedly polemical way. This Jesus is the Christ of Christians, but not necessarily the Messiah of historic Jewish expectation, although the Evangelist continues to think that Jews should accept him as such. The christological preaching or teaching of John is from here on the occasion for offense on the part of the Jews. It is not just that Jesus claims to be the Messiah, a claim they reject. What Jesus claims for himself strikes them as an intolerable offense. It looks like a denial of monotheism. Jesus' claim to be working still with the Father (John 5:17) is thus construed as a claim to be equal to God. In all probability this construal of Jesus' claim is in at least some sense correct, and is acknowledged by Christians to be so. Despite the fact that the claim that Jesus is making himself equal to God is a cause of the most profound offense, it is not denied or disclaimed outright. Indeed, rightly understood, it represents the distinctive christological confession that has arisen in the Johannine church.

Nevertheless, the claim is explained. Jesus does nothing that he has not seen the Father doing and claims nothing more than the Father has granted him (5:19-20). At the same time Jesus presents himself as the revelation of God, the eschatological salvation-bringer:

> Truly, truly, I say to you, he who hears my word and believes him who sent me, has eternal life; he does not come into judgment, but has passed from death to life. . . . For as the Father has life in himself, so he has granted the Son also to have life in himself. (5:24, 26)

The offense is qualified, explained, and later justified by appeal to witnesses: John the Baptist (5:33), Jesus' own works (5:36), the Father himself (5:37), the scriptures (5:39), and, therefore, Moses (5:45-46). But the offense remains. What is the meaning of the Baptist? What do Jesus' signs or works portend? Where is the Father's witness to be interpreted? All these questions are at issue in the interchange between the Johannine Christians and those with whom they debate. Because there is no agreement on any of them, there can be no agreement on the validity of the claims made by, or for, Jesus.

It is a matter of considerable historical import and interest whether, or to what extent, the claims made for Jesus in the first instance led to the polemical situation we find in the Fourth Gospel. Did the Christology expressed in the Johannine Gospel precede and give rise to the polemic? Or has that Christology evolved over a period of decades as questions and challenges to claims made in the name of Jesus resulted, not in the moderation of those claims, but in their accentuation or perhaps their qualification in ways that heightened rather than reduced the offense? I think the latter question more adequately describes the situation and that some such process is what we find reflected in John 5. In chapter 9 we find further clues as to how this polemical situation developed.[25]

Christology did not begin with Jesus' proclaiming himself, as he does in the Fourth Gospel. It began with Jesus' announcing God's salvation, the advent of his kingdom or rule. However else Jesus may have conceived of himself, he was certainly conscious of his role as the herald of that kingdom. The earliest church, composed of his disciples and others, proclaimed Jesus the Messiah at his resurrection. (If he thought of himself in such terms, he did not announce it publicly during his career.) Paul argues that in Jesus Christ God acts to pronounce the ungodly righteous while at the same moment revealing his wrath against human sin. The synoptic authors rework and arrange traditions originating in Jesus' historic ministry to present him as the fulfillment of emerging Christian conceptions of messianic expectation. These conceptions originated in Judaism and were mined out of the OT, the early Christians' Bible. Yet by and large they represented a reformulation of those expectations in the light of Christian perceptions of the significance of Jesus' career. As we see these formulations, in the NT at least, they are fundamentally conditioned or shaped by belief in Jesus' resurrection and in the saving effect of his death. More and more, salvation is found and proclaimed in him. There is a sense in which John represents the culmination of this tendency. He has set the developed Christology within the context of Jesus' historic ministry. Thus the Johannine Jesus is portrayed as performing those acts of judgment and salvation, that is, the giving of life, which had been the prerogative of God. They had been the primary object of expectation and hope for the eschatological future (5:25–27).

Not surprisingly, Jews, and quite possibly also Jewish Christians, found such talk dangerous and blasphemous. Jesus makes himself equal to God. Therefore, Jesus responds at length in John 5:30–47 to possible objections to the claims made for him, and his words sound like a rejoinder to objections already raised against him. Curiously, the Jewish objections to which Jesus speaks and the situation of opposition he describes here have not yet appeared in the narrative, but in the following chapters (esp. chaps. 6—10) they will be heard increasingly. It is almost as if we had dropped in on the middle of the dispute. The fundamental objection is that the Jesus of Christian confession and proclamation (not the historical Jesus) is an impostor for whom blasphemous claims are made (cf. 7:47; 8:48, 52; 10:20): "You, being a man, make yourself God" (10:33). Ultimately the Johannine Christian answer to this objection is to fly in the teeth of it:

> Jesus answered them, "Is it not written in your law, 'I said, you are gods'? If he called them gods to whom the word of God came (and scripture cannot be broken), do you say of him whom the Father consecrated and sent into the world, 'You are blaspheming,' because I said, 'I am the Son of God'? If I am not doing the works of my Father, then do not believe me; but if I do them, even though you do not believe me, believe the works, that you may know and understand that the Father is in me and I am in the Father." (10:34-38)

Yet the accusation that Jesus makes himself equal to God, or makes himself God, is not allowed to go unchallenged. At one point that is crucial for the Johannine Christians it is qualified. "I can do nothing on my own authority," says Jesus (John 5:30); "as I hear, I judge; and my judgment is just, because I seek not my own will but the will of him who sent me."

John 9

Because of its distinctly Johannine character and the way in which the dialogue builds upon the narrative, the story of the restoration of sight to the blind man (chap. 9) merits close attention. Moreover, such attention may shed light on how the vigorous polemic of chapter 5 developed.

The first paragraph (9:1–12) is in many respects similar to the synoptic miracle stories. The miracle is introduced with only the slightest connecting link with the preceding scene. Such a vague introduction is common in the synoptics. The idea that sickness or deformity is punishment for sin (vv. 2–3; cf. v. 34; Luke 13:1–5) is an ancient one, and although Jesus rejects it (v. 3), his own interpretation of the man's blindness is scarcely more acceptable to modern humanitarianism. He is blind so that the works of God may be manifest in him. Here is one of two remarkable parallels to chapter 11. In 11:4 the sickness of Lazarus is said to be for the glory of God and of the Son. The second parallel (9:4–5) is a subtle allusion to the coming death of Jesus and corresponds to 11:9–10. Already the inevitability of Jesus' death has been indicated by passing references of the Evangelist (2:22; 7:39) and by the attitude of the Jews in controversy with Jesus (5:18; 8:37, 40, 59). Now as the public ministry begins to move toward its conclusion, Jesus' last acts of healing are placed under the shadow of the cross.

That Jesus calls himself the light of the world (v. 5) shows the close connection between the prologue and the Gospel proper. Such a statement as, "I am the light of the world," belongs to a group of so-called "I am" sayings, which are distinctive of the Fourth Gospel (6:35; 10:11; 11:25; 14:6; 15:1). These sayings are typical and suitable expressions of the Johannine Jesus, who proclaims himself and his dignity. By contrast, in the synoptics, where he does not proclaim himself, but the kingdom of God, "I am" statements of this sort are seldom if ever found.

As in chapter 5, the miracle itself is described briefly and with restraint (vv. 6–7). In the synoptics also Jesus is said to heal with spittle (Mark 8:23; Matt. 9:27–32). The pool of Siloam, where Jesus sent the man to wash, has actually been located in modern times. Possibly for the Evangelist the most significant thing about the pool, however, was the meaning of its name, "sent." Throughout the Gospel Jesus is described as the one sent by God (e.g., 3:17). The man's obedience to Jesus and the results are described as succinctly as possible. The basic miracle story is actually much less elaborate and detailed than many similar stories in the synoptic tradition, perhaps an indication that John possessed a primitive miracle story in simple form. At least in this instance he seems not to have been interested in the details of the miracle although they are nevertheless recounted (but contrast 11:38–44).

We have already noticed passages (vv. 4–5; possibly v. 3) which are possibly examples of the Evangelist's own additions to this simple story. From v. 8 onward we lose track of the older story almost completely. From that point on there is a dialogue, mostly in Johannine style and principally concerned with questions fundamental to Johannine theology. Typically, Jesus does most of the talking.

We have seen much the same pattern of event plus interpretation in chapter 5. It appears also in chapter 6, and there is a variation upon it in chapter 11, where the traditional miracle story has apparently been interlaced with Johannine dialogue and discourse. Indeed, something of the same style may be seen also in chapters 3 (Nicodemus) and 4 (the Samaritan woman). In both instances an incident, a meeting between Jesus and another person, leads into a dialogue or a dialogue and discourse, and in each case the conversation develops just those themes that the Evangelist wishes to emphasize. On a smaller scale this occurs also in connection with the cleansing of the temple (2:13–22). On a considerably larger scale chapters 13 through 17 may be interpreted as conforming to this pattern. There the events of the Last Supper, especially the washing of the disciples' feet and the identification of Judas as the betrayer of Jesus, lead into an extensive dialogue and discourse. Again, something of the same phenomenon occurs in the trial scene, where the arraignment before Pilate, recounted in the synoptics, provides the occasion for a uniquely Johannine account of the conversation between Jesus and the Roman procurator. Even in the resurrection story (chap. 20) the Evangelist does not stop with an account of the empty tomb (Mark) or with a vision of the risen

Lord and a commission (Matthew and Luke). Instead, the risen Jesus engages in dialogue with Thomas, and his last word—actually the last word of the Gospel apart from the colophon—is his response to him (20:29). Again in the appendix (chap. 21) the same pattern appears, with Peter and Jesus engaged in conversation and Jesus' final word addressed to him.

The theological emphases of the synoptic Gospels are usually implicit in their choice, structure, and editing of the material. In John, however, such points become explicit and tend to occupy the center of the stage. The Evangelist wishes to make theological issues clear and at the same time show that they are rooted in the words and work of the historical Jesus. In John such issues, particularly Christology, usually become explicit in the narratives and in the words of Jesus. In our narrative, however, these issues emerge principally in the several interrogations of the blind man (9:8–12, 13–17, 18–23, 24–34) which follow the account of the healing. First, the man's neighbors question him (vv. 8ff.); next the Pharisees (vv. 13–17); then the man's parents are questioned by the Jews (vv. 18–23); finally, the Jews return to question the man himself a second time (vv. 24–34). In fact, this man is, uniquely, the hero of the episode.

In the brief narrative of the initial interrogation (vv. 8–12) we learn more of the healed man's background and hear of the astonishment and even disbelief of his neighbors (vv. 8–9). The man calmly and certainly identifies himself as the blind beggar whom they have known, and describes how and by whom he has been healed. As the story progresses, this modest but unwavering certainty is noteworthy. Here, as elsewhere, he possesses no theoretical or other knowledge about his benefactor except that the man called Jesus has healed him.

When brought before the Pharisees (vv. 13–17), the man's certainty and simplicity remain impressive (v. 15). For the first time we learn that the healing had been performed on the Sabbath day (v. 14), a common feature of the synoptic tradition, where Jesus is more than once accused of illegally performing healings—that is, working—on the Sabbath (cf. also John 5). Probably no significant distinction should be drawn between Pharisees and Jews in John. John's characteristic designation of those who oppose Jesus and his work is simply "the Jews." When he does mention a particular sect of Judaism it is generally the Pharisees. The reason for this may not be obvious, but if John was written after the Roman war (A.D. 70), the main Jewish opponents of Christianity could only have been Pharisees. The other principal sects, Sadducees, Zealots, and Essenes, had been either dissolved or sharply reduced in size and influence as a result of that conflict and its aftermath. When John portrays the Pharisees as leading the opposition to Jesus, this is a good indication that they were the group most actively competing with or opposing Christianity at the end of the first century. The disagreement among the Pharisees (v. 16) is typical of the division Jesus causes among people. Some reject him out of hand, because he violates their notions of what a holy or righteous man

must be: "He does not keep the Sabbath." Others are at least open to the testimony of his works, to see them as "signs," signifying who Jesus is. The
question is then put to the blind man: "What do you say about him, since he
has opened your eyes?" Earlier the man has simply spoken of "the man called
Jesus." Now he says that he is a prophet, that is, not a sinner as his detractors
contend but a man sent from God.

The mounting opposition to Jesus then takes the form of the Jews' refusal
to believe that the man had actually been born blind (v. 18); accordingly, his
parents are next called to testify (vv. 18–23). They are obviously anxious not
to involve themselves, but they do give a minimally truthful testimony. The
man who claims to have been healed by Jesus the prophet is, in fact, their son
who was born blind (v. 20). This, however, is as far as they are willing to go.
For all questions about how or by whom he was healed, the parents refer the
questioners back to their son (v. 21). The Evangelist now interjects an explanation of the reticence of the parents (vv. 22–23): They feared being put out of
the synagogue, because "the Jews" had already decided to expel from the synagogue anyone who confessed Jesus to be the Messiah. This explanation does
not really fit the time of Jesus, but rather the end of the first Christian century.
Again the key seems to be found in a crisis of Jewish-Christian relations that
immediately preceded the publication of the Gospel. After the destruction of
Jerusalem and the formation of the Jewish Council of Jamnia under Pharisaic
leadership, people were apparently being forced, or felt themselves forced, to
leave the synagogue for professing Christ.[26] The theme of excommunication
from the synagogue occurs more than once in John (12:42; 16:2; cf. Luke
6:22). Despite the parents' timidity, the attempt to discredit the claims of the
man, and indirectly to discredit Jesus, comes to grief on the hard fact that a
change has occurred in him. He was born blind, but is so no longer.

The same hearing continues and the man is called again (vv. 24ff.). The
opening statement scarcely encourages any hope that there will be an impar-
tial tribunal. Despite the lack of conclusive evidence against Jesus, the opposition to him has now hardened (v. 24). The serenity of the man healed contrasts
with the obviously hostile jury (v. 25). Rather than enter into a debate with
his questioners, he simply recites what he knows on the basis of what he has
experienced. This most effective and infuriating response (especially in view
of the failure to show that the man was not blind in the first place) drives the
questioners to take a new tack (v. 26). Their apparent attempt to get at the facts
may betray a suspicion that because Jesus has used spittle in the act of healing
he is therefore guilty of adopting the tricks of an illegal sorcerer. At this point
the man understandably shows signs of irritation (v. 27). His reply is intentionally cutting and draws a bitter retort (vv. 28–29). Of course, the Jews' claim
to be the true disciples of Moses is not accepted by the Evangelist (cf. 5:45–
47). That the healed man is Jesus' disciple has not heretofore been suggested.
Nevertheless, before the end it turns out to be true.

In v. 29, as throughout chapters 2—12, rejection of Jesus is based upon a religious certainty that refuses to question itself, a harking back to an earlier revelation that is now viewed as immutable law, admitting of no further clarification, alteration, or argument. That the Jews or Jesus' opponents do not know the origin of Jesus is altogether typical of John's thought. To know Jesus' true origin is to know that he is sent by God. The Jews ironically do not know the tragic truth of their observation that they are ignorant of Jesus' origin.[27] The man's response to those who see themselves as religious authorities (v. 30) is a classic reflection upon their capacity to judge Jesus. The didactic elaboration of the brusque retort (vv. 31–33) strikes home because it is based on presuppositions that the questioners turned accusers also share. The response of the man healed is so devastating that the only possible reaction is an outburst of angry frustration (v. 34). They cast him out—possibly out of the hearing room—but more probably out of the synagogue or the Jewish community (cf. vv. 22–23).

The latter interpretation accords with the remainder of the account (vv. 35ff.). After the man healed has been excommunicated from the synagogue because of his refusal to repudiate the one who healed him, Jesus himself returns to him. At this point the man appears to have no special theological knowledge of Jesus. In v. 35 we see one of the fairly numerous instances of the term *Son of man* in John's Gospel. As in the synoptics it usually appears on the lips of Jesus himself as a self-designation. Although in John it has lost much of its apocalyptic coloration (cf. Daniel 7), it is still a term of dignity, not of humiliation. The man's answer to Jesus' question is typically guileless (v. 36), and only now does Jesus reveal his full and true identity (v. 37). The man's response (v. 38) probably indicates that he understands Son of man to be a messianic title, although it could be translated, "Sir, I believe." In the synoptics the word can appear as such a polite form of address, *Milord,* or *Sir,* but here the meaning almost certainly goes beyond that. "Lord, I believe" is a christological confession, as is made plain by the statement that at this point the man worshiped Jesus. The final words of Jesus (vv. 39ff.), now addressed not so much to the man as to the total situation, are a commentary on his whole mission.[28]

The traces of Jewish-Christian polemic at the end of the first century already noted in this chapter lead us to suspect that the same situation is in view in the strange statement that Jesus has come in order that those who do not see may see and in order that those who see may become blind (v. 39). Those who do not see are obviously not the physically blind. The blindness and sight referred to here are of a different order. Jesus has said at the beginning of this story (v. 4), "I am the light of the world" (cf. also 1:4ff.; 8:12; 12:46). He gives sight to those in darkness, but those who try to walk by their own light are blinded. To receive sight, to see the true light, is to recognize one's condition of blindness. The Jews, who insist upon their prior revelatory knowledge ("we see") and their right to judge Jesus, become blind because of this pretension. Their rejection of Jesus proves their blindness, whereas their insistence that they see confirms their guilt (9:41). The pretension that one already sees prevents that self-knowledge and recognition of one's true condition that is the first step to genuine sight. So the effect of Jesus' appearance is to blind such people (v. 39), at least until they are ready to recognize their actual state.

Chapter 9 is a kind of paradigm of Jesus' public ministry, portraying in dramatic form the statement of the prologue that the light shines in darkness and the darkness has not comprehended (or "overcome") it (v. 5). Moreover, vv. 9–13 of the prologue take on concreteness and specificity in light of this story. It also represents a movement or progression in John's narration of Jesus' ministry. The hostility that has become evident already (cf. chaps. 5 and 8) could not be made plainer. Finally, this portrayal of Jesus as the giver of sight and, by implication, of light, prepares the way for the climactic manifestation of Jesus as the giver of life (chap. 11).

The principal point of the chapter does not lie in its contribution to historical knowledge of Jesus' ministry, despite the fact that a primitive, traditional story probably lies at the basis of the theological development. The questions addressed arise not out of Jesus' own time, but out of encounters between Christianity and Judaism or Christianity and the world. That this is no "spiritualizing" interpretation of the text, but represents the genuine intention of the author, is confirmed in the concluding word of Jesus (vv. 39ff.); in the terms of the narrative Jesus succinctly characterizes his whole mission.

Thus in this chapter John's distinctive view of Jesus as the light and life of mankind finds expression. The historical miracle is itself indispensable in that it manifests the fact that Jesus really changes men. The stubborn insistence of the healed man upon the fact of his healing bears eloquent testimony to this. He grounds his relation to Jesus on what has actually happened to him, even though he cannot give this experience adequate expression until Jesus reveals himself to him. In the end he acknowledges and worships the Christ whose reality and activity on his behalf he has already felt. Although the Johannine Christology is here in evidence, it lies somewhat in the background. In the foreground is soteriology (the concept of salvation and its effect)—not so much who Jesus is, but what he does. In fact, who he is becomes known through, and is grounded upon, what he does. As Jesus here manifests himself as the light of the world by giving sight to the blind, so in chapter 11 he appears as the resurrection and the life by raising the dead.

The fact that the specific doctrine of Christ and Jesus himself remain somewhat in the background suggests another observation. There is a sense in which the real hero of the story is the nameless man who is healed. He becomes a model of the Jew who stubbornly clings to his confession of Jesus despite the hostility of his compatriots. The heroic character of the man healed is a feature of this particular miracle story as of no other in John. Certainly neither the restored man of chapter 5 nor even Lazarus in chapter 11 emerges as a hero. The ruler of 4:46–54 comes off well, as in the synoptic parallels, but his character is not displayed and developed in the same way. If Jesus had not reappeared at the end of chapter 9 to confirm the man in his new-found faith and to pronounce a final interpretative word over the whole affair, one might have thought that after the brief account of the miracle Jesus simply faded out of the picture, except as he was present in his embryonic disciple.

Although there is no exact parallel to this feature in a Johannine miracle story, the account does bring to light an important Johannine characteristic— namely, the author's interest in the various types of people who confront Jesus. Whatever one may think about the historical basis of such stories of John, they clearly possess historical verisimilitude, although many of the characters who encounter Jesus are typical and perhaps symbolic. There is Nathanael, the true Israelite in whom there is no guile (1:47ff.). There is Nicodemus, the teacher of Israel, who at first cannot comprehend Jesus and yet later defends him and finally returns to help bury him (3:1ff.; 7:50; 19:39). In contrast to Nicodemus is the nameless Samaritan woman, the representative of a heterodox Judaism (4:7ff.). Yet if the characters are symbolic, they are also lifelike. In chapter 11 Mary and Martha, along with the wily Caiaphas, stand out as real people. And even Pontius Pilate shows a touch of humanity in the passion narrative (18:28ff.). Although the disciples do not appear in the farewell discourse except to ask questions, their questions are understandable in view of the total picture that John has painted. Thus Thomas' question (14:5) contributes to the traditional portrayal of him as "doubting Thomas." With the exception of Peter, and perhaps James and John, in the synoptics the disciples are shadowy characters. By contrast, in John some of these disciples play significant roles (for example, Philip, Thomas, Lazarus, and Nathanael), but James and John are not mentioned by name.

Pre-eminent among the disciples in the Fourth Gospel is, of course, the unnamed Beloved Disciple, certainly an exemplary figure among Jesus' circle of disciples. As we have seen there is no firm basis in the Gospel for the traditional identification of this disciple with John, the son of Zebedee. Alternatively, the Beloved Disciple has been identified with Lazarus by some interpreters, whereas others have insisted that he is a composite, ideal figure, and not any single historical person. The objection that John would not have invented such a person may be met by the rejoinder that we cannot prove that John did not invent any number of the characters in the Gospel, about whom we know nothing either from the synoptics or from any other source. Here, as at so many points, John alternately mystifies and tantalizes the reader and defies the historical investigator.

The story of the healing of the blind man mirrors both the characteristics and the perplexities of the Fourth Gospel. We find here a true-to-life picture of how people react when older orthodoxies are confronted by new claims and a remarkably lifelike and sympathetic picture of the man whom Jesus healed. In and behind this scene there appears John's understanding of the nature and work of Jesus Christ, as well as the actual experience of those who confessed Christ in a hostile environment. Yet for all that the portrait of Jesus lacks the humanity of the other characters. This is all the more surprising in view of the intensely human—if authoritative—Jesus who emerges at many points in the synoptic account. The Johannine Jesus by contrast behaves strangely by human standards (2:4; 7:2–10; 11:6). This state of affairs is enough to set us on our guard against reading John as a historical book in any ordinary sense. It is generally less so than the other Gospels. John's portrayal of Jesus is not designed to represent his humanity for the benefit of our curiosity and to make him personally more familiar. Rather, as in the prologue he speaks of Jesus as the Word or revelation of God, so in the body of the Gospel he speaks of the Word of God under the form of Jesus of Nazareth. Although he does not deny that Jesus was really man, his primary interest and emphasis is focused upon his conviction that through him God is speaking to man. The single-mindedness of this theological concept is etched sharply against the background of John's perceptive presentation of humanity in all its color and concreteness. At this he is a master, and it is nowhere more apparent than in the story of the man blind from birth.

The texts we have examined in this chapter present two historical levels, that of Jesus and that of the Christian community which confesses him to be the Christ. If anything, it is the latter level which seems closer to us and has on critical reflection the clearer aspect of authenticity.

CHAPTER FIVE

THE JOHANNINE PERSPECTIVE: THE PRESENT, CHRISTIAN DIMENSION (CHAPTERS 16 AND 1 JOHN 1)

The substance of the Gospel of John is explicitly Christian in a sense that even the synoptic Gospels are not. That is, in John Jesus utters the Christian confession or credo and places himself, his person as well as his work, at the center of his teaching. Chapter 16 and the farewell discourses (chaps. 14—16) generally are even more distinctively Christian than the rest of the Gospel, for here Jesus in speaking to his disciples anticipates their situation after he has departed from them. Thus in effect he speaks to the post-resurrection church. The problems addressed are uniquely and explicitly Christian. Jesus, by the device of describing in advance the future situation, addresses the present existence of Johannine Christians, and so the present Christian moment or dimension of the Fourth Gospel emerges in complete clarity. The farewell discourses are set in the context of Jesus' last meal with his disciples (chap. 13), familiar from the synoptics. They conclude with his lengthy prayer (chap. 17), which is uniquely and distinctively Johannine.

The apocalyptic discourses of Matthew, Mark, and Luke are the synoptic counterparts of Johannine farewell discourses, and there is a sense in which they too address the situation of the post-resurrection church. But the differences are typical and quite significant. The synoptic discourses deal with the events and signs which are to mark the continuing unfolding of history, that is, the apocalyptic drama, both outside and within the Christian community. The culmination is the arrival of the Son of man. They are composed of sayings of Jesus, which if not authentic are clearly traditional. They bear the imprint of material which has been handed down. The Johannine discourses, on the other hand, deal with the disciples' or the community's relationship to Jesus as it will be reconstituted after his death. Eschatology is reinterpreted. Jesus is no longer the Son of man who is to arrive at some point of time in the future. He is to come to his disciples immediately and to abide with them. Thus Jesus no longer speaks about an apocalyptic drama involving nations and world history, but about relations within the Christian community, the church. If there are traditional words of Jesus embedded in the Johannine discourses, they have been radically reminted or reinterpreted, even as the eschatological perspective has been revised.

Chapter 16

It is difficult to break up chapters 15—16 even for purposes of analysis, since the several various themes and emphases interlock. By looking rather closely at chapter 16 we may, however, identify the principal points made by Jesus in the farewell discourses.

In 16:1–4 Jesus concludes his discussion of the hatred of the world for the disciples which began in 15:18 (cf. also the reprise in 17:14). The effects of this hatred are now specified (16:2): they will be put out of synagogues (cf. 9:22; 12:42) and even killed. As we have already seen the threat of expulsion from the synagogues envisions a situation in which Jews who confessed Jesus as the Christ were excluded from the fellowship of the Jewish community. This was apparently an important, if not epoch-making, turning point in the history of the Johannine Christian community. Followers of Jesus in this and other Christian communities did not originally intend that by confessing Jesus to be the Christ (or Messiah) of Jewish expectation they should cease to be Jews. Jesus himself never thought of giving up Judaism to found a new religion. Paul, when he wants to speak of the person who is obedient to God, writes: "He is a *Jew* who is one inwardly . . . his praise is not from men but from God" (Rom. 2:29). The Johannine community has within its vivid recollection experienced the trauma of expulsion from the house of Israel. What is anticipated as a fearful consequence in 9:22 and 12:42 is firmly predicted in 16:2, which doubtless describes the situation of the Christian circles which produced the Gospel.

Whether or not Jewish Christians were also executed or subject to fear of execution by their fellow Jews, as 16:2 may be taken to imply, is an important question. That such a mortal threat did not lie outside the realm of possibility may also be inferred from John's portrayal of the deadly hostility of the Jews to Jesus. Such descriptions may in fact reflect a continuing mortal hatred toward Jesus' emissaries. The Jewish character of the opposition seems to be implicit in the belief of those who kill Christians that they are "offering service to God." (The Greek term *latreia* is a common one for worship.) On the other hand, Christians were widely considered impious or atheists by their pagan contemporaries, and the statement in question may simply refer— admittedly in Jewish or Christian terms—to the religious reasons for persecuting Christians. It is difficult to say on the basis of our rather fragmentary and allusive evidence whether Jews were, in fact, subjecting Johannine Christians to mortal threat. Yet in view of the harshly polemical tone displayed on both sides in the Gospel debates between Jesus and the Jews, that possibility must be taken seriously.[29].

In any event a growing hostility between Jews and Christians is reflected at this and other points in the Gospel. Doubtless that hostility and conflict played a significant role in the development of the Christian consciousness which produced the Fourth Gospel. The separation from the synagogue quite clearly lies in the Johannine community's past. Otherwise the strong sense of the demarcation of the community from the world, and particularly from the Jews, would be difficult to understand. A sectarian self-consciousness is strongly reflected in the dualism of the Johannine writings and in the awareness that, unlike the synagogue and the world, they believe in and belong to Jesus.[30]

Yet the opponents, the outsiders, are not only, or at least not necessarily Jews. In v. 3 Jesus says that the murderous opposition he has just described springs from not knowing the Father or himself (obviously an ignorance of his true origin, goal, and nature). This description would, on Johannine terms, apply to other unbelievers and opponents than Jews. Whether or not such heathen rejection of the gospel and its representatives is envisioned is debatable, but the description is principally appropriate. Moreover, the opposition is initially described as the *world's* hatred (15:18–19). Jewish rejection or persecution of Jesus and his followers is apparently the archetype of the world's opposition; in fact, in surrendering itself to Caesar Judaism becomes the world (19:15). But the world's opposition is not limited to Judaism, although the Jews have become representative of the world. It is thus accurate to say that in John the Jews represent the world, but wrong to discount the role which the synagogue and certain Jews have actually played in the evolution of Johannine theology and styles of speech. A genuine church-synagogue dialogue and conflict underlies the Fourth Gospel.

Apparently vv. 1 and 4 serve to frame the important word of 16:2–3 and to call attention to the setting and purpose for which it is intended. Jesus speaks of things which the church will remember and appreciate only in the light of its subsequent, post-resurrection history (cf. 2:17, 22; 7:39; 12:16). Indirectly, Christians are admonished to take note of Jesus' predictions (16:4). The motif of the importance of the disciples' later recollection and interpretation of events and Jesus' word is an important one in the Gospel, particularly in the farewell discourses, as an examination of the rest of this chapter will confirm.

In 16:4b one can discern John's recognition and understanding of the fact that the things he portrays Jesus as saying on the eve of his departure were not part of the message of Jesus during his public ministry. It was not necessary for Jesus to explain some things to his followers while he himself was still with them. Now, however, he leaves them to go to the Father. The question which Jesus says none of his disciples is asking him (16:5) has in effect been asked in 14:5. Perhaps this seeming anomaly is to be explained by the fact that two independent farewell discourses (chap. 14; chaps. 15—16) have been conjoined in the final redaction of the Gospel. Alternatively, this anomaly may function as a means of returning to the theme of chapter 14. Jesus departs from his disciples, and his departure is the cause of perplexity and even sorrow. The discourses are intended to explain his departure and allay such feelings of despair.

What then is the meaning of Jesus' departure? First of all, which departure is referred to? The departure, and absence of Jesus after his death, that is, between his death and resurrection appearances, or after his resurrection, that is, the ascension? Verse 7 seems to indicate that the latter is primarily in view, for only after the resurrection does the Spirit come (20:22; cf. 7:39). Traditionally in early Christian thought the Spirit appears in the time between the resurrection and the parousia. The word "Counselor" in the RSV translates the Greek *parakletos*.[31] He is the Spirit of truth (15:26; 16:13) or the Holy Spirit (14:26). The exact meaning of this term in John, or why John uses this particular term of the Holy Spirit in the discourses, has never been satisfactorily determined. In the KJV and RV it was translated as "Comforter." In 1 John 2:1 the term is used of Jesus, and in the RSV is translated "Advocate," which corresponds to its etymological and generally accepted meaning. NEB adopts this translation in the Gospel as well. It is at least partially justified by the fact that at the first mention of the Paraclete (14:16) he is called "another paraclete," an expression that seems to take up the understanding of Jesus as Paraclete/advocate found in 1 John 2:1. To some extent the translation "advocate" suits the function of Jesus in the Fourth Gospel, especially the farewell discourses. Jesus is the advocate of his disciples before the Father (cf. chap. 17). Yet it remains a question whether this term adequately covers every function as it is set forth there.

Doubtless because of the immediately preceding discussion of the world's hatred, the relation of the Paraclete to the world comes under consideration (vv. 8-11). In effect his work is to expose and condemn the error and sinfulness of the world in rejecting Jesus. But by and large the interest in the work of the Paraclete vis-à-vis the world is secondary. In the main John is concerned with the way the Paraclete functions in the church, that is, in relation to the disciples. To this theme, so characteristic of the farewell discourses, Jesus turns again in 16:12-15.

The most startling aspect of what is now said about the Spirit of truth concerns his revelatory function. At first it appears that the Spirit of truth is to give the disciples additional revelations (vv. 12-13). The notion of the Spirit's bringing additional revelations, or of the risen, exalted Jesus' giving additional revelations through the Spirit, was not uncommon in early Christianity as the Book of Revelation, chapters 1—3, clearly shows. Moreover, even Paul has words of the Lord Jesus that are given him through direct revelation or inspiration rather than by tradition (2 Cor. 12:8-9). The potential danger of such claims to unique, personal revelations is not hard to see. Therefore, "spirits" must be tested to see whether they are from God (1 John 4:1; cf. 1 Thess. 5:21). Doubtless the authors of the Gospel of John and the Johannine letters lived in a Christian community, or communities, in which Spirit-inspired utterances were not uncommon. Their potential danger was real, but they were not to be simply suppressed or rejected. There existed criteria by which the validity of revelations or "spirits" could be judged (1 John 4:1-3). In the farewell discourses Jesus himself makes clear that the Spirit does not reveal any and every sort of thing. That he does not speak on his own authority

(16:13) means that what he has the right to say and reveal is subject to the authority of Jesus. He utters what he hears—from Jesus—and "declares the things that are to come." That is, the Spirit of prophecy speaks only on Jesus' authority even while he interprets the unfolding future to the community of his followers.[32] At this point there seem to be striking parallels between the utterances of Jesus in the farewell discourses and the way the Lord, the Spirit, and the prophet relate to each other and function in the Book of Revelation (esp. chaps. 1—3). While it is very plain that the Spirit's role is to expound to the community the revelation given in Jesus, it is not so obvious how that revelation in Jesus is understood and what this unfolding of that revelation really amounts to.

Although John makes very clear that the Spirit only speaks on Jesus' authority, taking what is Jesus' and declaring it to the disciples (or the church), it remains a question how "what is mine" (that is, Jesus') is understood in relation to the historical Jesus and the tradition about him. Quite possibly the key is found in v. 15, "all that the Father has is mine." Revelations of the Spirit which are authentically God-given are also from Jesus. Thus all true Spirit-inspired revelation glorifies Jesus and is the declaration of his truth. To say this, however, is not helpful in solving the problem of distinguishing authentic from inauthentic spirits or revelations. But perhaps just because the problem is left unresolved in the Fourth Gospel it must be dealt with in 1 John!

When one reviews all the Paraclete sayings (14:15-17, 25-26; 15:26-27; 16:12-15) and related passages, however, it is evident that the Evangelist does not wish to say simply that every true revelation of God is a revelation of Jesus without in any way specifying what Jesus may or may not be or represent. The Spirit bears witness to Jesus (15:26), who is clearly understood to be a historical figure out of the past. He brings to *remembrance* all Jesus has said to his disciples (14:26). Earlier on the importance of the disciples' retrospectively recalling and understanding what Jesus has said to them is underlined (2:17, 22; 12:16). John does not wish to say that every revelation from God is a revelation of Jesus without indicating what may be a revelation of God. It is, in fact, Jesus who defines a revelation from God. He is God's revelation (*logos*), and Jesus is clearly understood to be a concrete historical figure who among other things reveals that God is love (3:16), loves his own (13:1), and commands that they love one another (13:34-35). He is not anything anybody wants to make him. Nevertheless, the question of how the continuing revelation of God in Jesus relates to the historical Jesus in the author's own understanding remains. That problem is plainly evident in the very considerable difference between John and the synoptics, in which the tradition of Jesus, particularly Jesus' words, has not to any comparable degree been suffused with Christian theological and polemical interests, as well as Christian piety and spirituality.

It is by no means unreasonable to surmise that the specific function of the Spirit-Paraclete as described in the Fourth Gospel is actually represented in the figure and words of the Johannine Jesus. Not only the Christ-Jewish polemic of the first-century community and the accompanying Christian confession of Jesus comes to expression in John. Also inspired utterances of those empowered by the Spirit to speak in his name, and in the first person, are reflected in this Gospel.[33] Ample parallels and supporting evidence for this view can be found in 1 John and Revelation, not to mention Paul and other early Christian writings such as the Didache and Melito of Sardis.

There is in vv. 16–24 a rather long discussion of the saying of Jesus about "a little while," found in vv. 16 and 19. The saying occurs also in another form in 14:19. Related sayings appear in 7:33–34; 8:21; 12:35 and 13:33. At the root of such passages there is doubtless a traditional word of Jesus, well-known in Johannine circles. The sayings in 7:33–34; 8:21; and 12:35 speak of, or allude to, the departure of Jesus only and are addressed to the Jews or to the public; the same is true of 13:33, which although addressed to the disciples refers to what Jesus has said previously to the Jews. The problem of the authenticity of this saying, or some form of it, need not concern us. Our question has to do with its meaning at this point in the Gospel. As the questioning of the disciples develops (vv. 17–18) and Jesus renders a rather enigmatic answer (vv. 19ff.), one of two possible interpretations of the text must be chosen. Here the question becomes, is Jesus talking about his departure in death and return in the resurrection, or is he talking about his departure at the ascension and his return at the end of history? Presumably the former. The parousia interpretation seems already excluded by the statement of Judas in 14:22 and Jesus' answer, which confirms its correctness. Moreover, the disciples' sorrow, contrasted with the world's rejoicing (v. 20) is apparently a reference to divergent reactions to the crucifixion of Jesus. The apparent allusion to prayer in Jesus' name (vv. 23, 26–27) has in view the post-resurrection time of the church rather than the parousia. The references to seeing Jesus again (16:16, 19) then apply to his resurrection appearances.

Nevertheless, the parousia of Jesus is also indirectly in view, for one purpose of the farewell discourses is to assure the disciples that they will not be left alone in the world (14:18). This purpose hovers in the background of our text. Jesus appears to his disciples after his death, but these appearances terminate. John knows this from common Christian tradition. When they do, Christians are not left to face the world alone. Jesus continues to be with them through the Spirit, even though he does not appear to them. They can now pray to the Father in Jesus' name and he will hear (16:23, 26–27). Thus Jesus' departure to the Father from whom he came (16:28; cf. 17:8; 5:19) is grounds for his disciples' rejoicing. Because he goes away the Counselor or Paraclete (16:7), who represents an extension and continuation of the revelation of God in Jesus, comes.

At first glance the promise of 16:25 may seem more naturally to refer to the return of Jesus, that is, his parousia. Yet as we have already noted, the discussion of the disciples' praying "in the hour" indicates among other things that the time of the church is in view. The speaking in figures to which Jesus alludes (v. 25) refers to the discussion which has immediately preceded (vv. 16–24); the plain speaking which he promises actually occurs in v. 28. The response of the disciples (vv. 29–30), "Ah, now you are speaking plainly, not in any figure . . ." confirms this. The farewell discourses end with Jesus' speaking the truth plainly to his disciples and their comprehending.

Just at that point, however, Jesus expresses a curious reservation about their belief (vv. 31–32). How is this to be accounted for? In part by tradition. The abandonment of Jesus by his disciples after his arrest and arraignment is thoroughly fixed in the memory and traditions of early Christianity (cf. Mark 14:27, 50). Although in Mark it is embodied in an OT quotation (Zech. 13:7), in all probability it has a historical basis, for Christians would not likely have contrived a story so unflattering to the disciples. Nevertheless, this seems a strange place for John to introduce the tradition. Jesus has just spoken plainly to the disciples and they have professed to understand him. Then quite suddenly and for no apparent reason Jesus abruptly calls their understanding in question.

The solution to this seeming puzzle is probably to be found in the peculiar perspective of the Fourth Gospel. Throughout the Gospel Jesus himself speaks in Christian, confessional terms with a full knowledge of what is about to transpire. In the farewell discourses this knowledge applies particularly to the Johannine Christian church. The disciples, on the other hand, although they recognize Jesus for who he is when they first meet him (chap. 1) and are said to believe in him after his first public act (2:11), maintain and in the farewell discourses still manifest an ignorance about the most important matters (14:5ff.). In this respect the Johannine portrayal of the disciples before the crucifixion and resurrection is not unlike the Markan.[34] Thus even at this point Jesus points to and reflects upon the significant, residual admixture of unbelief that colors and taints the disciples' profession of their faith in him. While he speaks with full Christian knowledge, that is, knowledge that reflects the historical and doctrinal data on which Christian faith is built, they lack such knowledge and are unable to digest it even when Jesus expounds it to them. Such knowledge, the author knows, is inappropriate to them until they have known Jesus' crucifixion and experienced the reality of his resurrection (cf. esp. 20:26–29).

Jesus concludes the discourse by telling his disciples that he has spoken as he has that they may have peace (16:33; cf. the peace Jesus bestows in 14:27). But his words are not so much an explanation they can immediately assimilate as a heritage upon which they shall draw. His final statement ("In the world you have tribulation; but be of good cheer, I have overcome the world") is a word of realism and hope. Troubles are as real as the world is, but the disciples are not to be dismayed. They shall remain in the world (17:15), but not be overcome by it; for Jesus in apparently succumbing to the world's judgment of him has really judged (12:31–32; cf. 3:17–19; 16:8–11) and overcome the world.

1 John 1

The Gospel of John was written from the standpoint of Jesus' ministry, but it reaches into the post-resurrection period, into the time of the church, in ways that we have seen. The Johannine letters, on the other hand, are written from the standpoint of a community of Christians, the post-resurrection church, but reach back to the time of Jesus. The difference is significant and characteristic. The Gospel of John sees the ministry of Jesus from the perspective of the later church. First John wishes to put the situation of the later church under the perspective of Jesus' ministry. The character and intention of 1 John is fully apparent in its first chapter, which falls into two parts: 1:1–4 and vv. 5–10.

Although 2 and 3 John are clearly letters with epistolary salutations and conclusions (cf. the Pauline letters), 1 John is not. Yet it is clearly a written communication to a group of Christians from a leader (cf. 2:1), and we therefore with good reason refer to it as an epistle, or letter. The author of 2 and 3 John identifies himself as "the Elder" in the salutation. It has long been presumed, on the basis of language, style, and theological themes, that the same author wrote all three. This may or may not be true. Whether this author (or one of these authors) also wrote the Gospel of John is a good question. While there are certainly reasons for believing that the same author wrote all the letters as well as the Gospel, there are also reasons against common authorship. But we need not, and indeed cannot, adjudicate such matters in advance of an examination of the text, if at all.

The common authorship—or at least the common viewpoint of the Gospel and 1 John—is suggested by the very first verse. The Gospel's "in the beginning" is matched by 1 John's "that which was from the beginning." In both Gospel and Epistle the subject is ultimately Jesus Christ, who has become flesh. "The word became flesh and dwelt among us" (John 1:14) is one of the most theologically pregnant statements in all of Christian scripture. The prologue of the Gospel builds toward that climactic statement. That of 1 John, so to speak, begins with it. In fact, what most Christian readers have taken to be the meaning and significance of John 1:14 is spelled out with unmistakable clarity in 1 John 1:1. The Word's becoming flesh was a tangible and visible historical person and event. Because it has been seen witnesses can proclaim the life made manifest in him (1:2). The "word of life" (v. 1) is "the life" (v. 2) which has been made manifest, and that is clearly Jesus. Like the prologue of the Gospel, that of the Epistle holds the name of Jesus in reserve until the end (John 1:17; 1 John 1:3). In the Gospel the goal of the manifestation of the Word as life is described as belief (1:12); in 1 John it is described as fellowship (or communion, 1:3). This fellowship is first of all "with the Father and with his Son Jesus Christ," derivatively with the author and the Christian community he represents. The author writes, as he puts it, to complete the joy of both in this fellowship.

As closely allied as the prologue of 1 John seems to be with the prologue of the Gospel there is already a significant difference. The "beginning" (Greek, *arche*) of which the Gospel speaks is cosmic. It is the primordial state before the creation, in which the Word existed alongside God and in due course became his instrument in creation. Although the incarnation of the Word is suggested already in 1:5ff., particularly to anyone already familiar with the Christian story, it is not until 1:14 that it is clearly announced.

The beginning of 1 John 1:1, on the other hand, is apparently the historic beginning of the Christian gospel, that is, the good news of Jesus Christ. The phrase "from the beginning" (*ap'arches*) could be an allusion to the cosmic beginning of the Gospel. But in 2:7 and 3:11 exactly the same phrase is used in a clear and explicit reference to Jesus or the beginning of the Christian tradition. In 1 John 1:1 itself the phrase occurs in a context in which emphasis falls on the primary, or primal, experience of the historical incarnation. Probably "that which was from the beginning" refers to the beginning of the historic tradition, that is, to Jesus. Certainly such an interpretation is in accord with the entire context of 1 John 1:1–4. It is as if the Epistle's focus on the Gospel prologue's message has been narrowed to 1:14, and the phrase, "the Word became flesh and dwelt among us" has been unfolded with particular emphasis upon its tangible and visible reality. Thus, the author of 1 John roots his message in Jesus, even as the author of the Gospel set Jesus in the context of the issues that confronted his own community.

The second half of 1 John 1 does not so clearly evoke the prologue of the Gospel, although its themes of light and darkness are touched upon in v. 5. There the message that God is light is, significantly, traced to Jesus. "The message we have heard from him" is obviously the message of Jesus. Of course, it is also the message about Jesus, that is, the Christian gospel. For the Johannine author(s) there is no distinction, as is clear from the Gospel, where Christology becomes the subject of Jesus' proclamation. The message that God is light, and totally so, not darkness at all, is a major premise of 1 John. We know it, of course, from the Gospel. Yet in the Epistle there is a subtle and significant difference in emphasis, for very quickly this light-darkness dualism becomes the basis for ethical exhortation (vv. 6–10).

The possibility of walking in darkness is next introduced (v. 6). To walk in darkness is to give the lie to any claim of fellowship with him. "Him" here presumably means Jesus, although it could (and should) mean God, the nearest antecedent of the pronoun. Yet "he is in the light" in v. 7 is apparently a reference to Jesus, not God, who is himself light; and this "he" is the same as the "him" of v. 6. So to say one has fellowship with Jesus and to walk in darkness is a lie and not to live according to the truth. Now the dualism of truth-lie interlocks with that of light-darkness. Of course, to be in the light is to be true, while to be in darkness is to be false. To walk in the light (v. 7) is to have fellowship with one another. Obviously, then, to walk in darkness (v. 6) is not to have such fellowship. Walking in light or in darkness are clearly alternative ways of living in relation to one's fellows. In 2:10–11 this is made quite explicit: "He who loves his brother abides in the light, and in it (or him) there is no cause for stumbling. But he who hates his brother is in the darkness and walks in darkness, and does not know where he is going, because the darkness has blinded his eyes."

It is altogether typical of 1 John that he first brings up the polarity of light and darkness and refers to existence in one or the other in more or less enig-matic ways. Later on he returns to it and makes more explicit what is meant. (2:10–11). But in 1:7 the author abruptly breaks away from the light-darkness and truth-falsehood dualism to speak of the redemptive work of Jesus: "the blood of Jesus his Son cleanses us from all sin." This is traditional Christian language and conceptuality. It has been so for nearly two millenia, and doubt-less already was so at the time John wrote. We shall return to the question of why he introduces it at just this point. For the moment we should observe that the idea that Christ's death removed sin is found in the other Gospels, in Paul, in Hebrews, and probably in John 1:29. It may also be inferred from John's account of Jesus' washing the disciples' feet. But the belief that Christ's blood cleanses from sin is more central to 1 John than to the Gospel.

From vv. 8–10 we can see why the cleansing power of Jesus' blood is men-tioned. Twice in quick succession the author refers to saying (or to those who say) "we have no sin" (vv. 8, 10). In each case he makes clear that to say or think this is a delusion. In the first he describes this as being deceived, in the second as lying. In the first case "the truth is not in us" if such a thing is said; in the second "we make him a liar and his word is not in us."

How is he made a liar? This is not obvious. First of all, it is Jesus who is made a liar. The pronouns refer back to Jesus Christ his Son (v. 8). Perhaps it is because God has sent Jesus to deal with the factual condition of sin, to deny this condition is to make him, or Jesus, a liar. In any event, if one will but confess sin, "he is faithful and just to forgive us our sins. . . ."

The emphasis on forgiveness continues in the succeeding chapter, as the author addresses his readers as "my little children." He writes so that they may not sin, but if anyone does, "we have an advocate with the Father," Jesus Christ (2:1). (The word translated "advocate" is *parakletos*; its technical meaning is "Advocate," which works much better here than in the Gospel, where RSV translates it "Counselor.") Jesus is the *expiation* for sins, "ours" (Christians', members of the Johannine community) and those of the whole world (v. 2). Cleansing from sin depends on knowing Christ, needless to say, and to know him is to keep his commandments (v. 3). The letter's line of thought runs from one key idea to another in a kind of logical progression, but without a structure that is entirely clear.

There is a dual stress on both the reality of sin and Christ's availability and ability to deal with it. There is no need to be overcome by sin, and the believer will not be overcome with sin unless he denies its existence, fails to confess it, does not allow Christ to cleanse him from it. To be assured of Christ's cleansing work, one must know him and follow his commands. As will become clearer in the course of the letter, Christ's commandment is essentially the command to love. The dual emphasis seems to address a situation in which sin is denied rather than confessed. Apparently there are believers, church members known to John, who by denying their sin cut themselves off from the cleansing power of Christ. It is not the case that John is indifferent to sin or soft on sin. He wants sin expunged from among the Christians to whom he writes. Nevertheless, to deny sin is not the same as to be cleansed from it and to confuse one with the other is fatal. At this stage of the letter John appeals to his readers not to allow themselves to fall into that confusion. It is altogether likely that he knows of Christians who have. Others come into the picture later on who not only live in mortal error and confusion, but encourage others to do so as well (3:7).

Several significant and essential aspects of Johannine Christianity reflected in 1 John have come into clear focus in this passage.

First, there is a common theological language, a common set of theological concepts and way of thinking shared with the Fourth Gospel: life and death, light and darkness, truth and falsehood, Jesus Christ as the Word of God. Jesus is the source of life, as well as light and truth. Typically, Jesus as the revelation of God and source of salvation and the images or symbols used to describe him are set in sharp contrast to their opposites: darkness, falsehood, and later on in the letter the antichrist. Thus the well-known Johannine dualism. So much common ground with the Gospel of John makes the theory of common authorship a reasonable conclusion, whether or not it is historically accurate.

Second, the Gospel prologue's emphasis on the manifestation of the Word in flesh, on the plane of historical reality, is heartily seconded in 1 John. In fact, as we have seen, 1 John seems to lift out and underscore the tangibility, visibility, and thus the corporeality of what has come to be called the doctrine of the incarnation. It may be that readers have seen this doctrine so clearly in the Gospel because it is underscored so heavily in the letter. On good grounds it is even suggested that the author of the letter wrote as he did so that no one would mistake what was intended in the Gospel. (Whether the author of the Epistle goes beyond, or intensifies, the meaning of the Gospel at this point is a valid question.) In this respect, however, as in the case of theological language and conceptuality, the Gospel of John and 1 John are closely related, if not identical.

A third feature of 1 John goes beyond what is found in the Gospel, however. The emphasis on Christ's blood, on its cleansing power, on Christ as expiation for sin (Greek, *hylasmos;* cf. *hylasterion* in Rom. 3:25) is a distinctive feature of 1 John. Although there are hints of this doctrine in the Fourth Gospel, there is not a comparable emphasis upon it. In this and several other respects (see below, pp. 12–14) the Epistle differs from the Gospel.

This leads to a fourth point. The emphasis on Christ's dealing with sin and the urgent call to admit and confess sins implies that there are those who do not, or who are in danger of failing to do so. This is the first hint of a thread that runs throughout 1 John. To be more accurate, it is part of the warp or woof of the letter. There is opposition, either experienced or anticipated, to the positions of the author at a number of points. On the basis of the tradition, which he takes to be received from Jesus (thus the emphasis on the *beginning*), John sets his position out, well aware that there are some who do not accept it, or do not accept his interpretation of it. Even the nature of the origin of the tradition, that is, Jesus himself, may be in dispute. In 1 John 4:1–3 the author enjoins the readers to test the spirits to distinguish whether they are from God or are false. Apparently the test is confessional. Whoever confesses Jesus Christ has come in the flesh is of God. Whoever denies it is not of God. There are Christians in John's purview, perhaps in churches for which he feels responsibility, who deny the fleshliness or humanity of Jesus. This denial, which became common in second-century Christianity, is known as docetism. Docetism was later condemned as heretical by church councils, and here we find 1 John already facing and condemning something rather like it.

Probably opposition to docetism, or docetic Christology, accounts for the emphatic insistence on the tangible reality of the Word of life, that is, Jesus, which we have already observed in the prologue of 1 John (1:1–4). Quite possibly the strange emphasis on Jesus Christ's having come by blood as well as water means that the death of Jesus, as well as his appearance and baptism, is an essential aspect of God's revelation. Therefore, through his death Jesus Christ's humanity is once again underscored.

Whether all the opposition John describes or anticipates is embodied in the same people or group is a good question, to which we shall never have an historically certain answer. A version of Christianity which denies the genuine humanity of Jesus, claims to be sinless, denies the saving efficacy of Jesus' death because it denies sin as well as the reality of that death, rejects obedience to the commandments of the earthly Jesus, and derives its authority from the Spirit directly is historically plausible. It cannot be demonstrated, only suggested, on the basis of 1 John. Although such a Christianity may have been without precedent, its later manifestations, whether ancient or modern, are obvious.

It is sometimes argued that the kind of docetic and Gnostic Christianity opposed in 1 John is also encountered and rejected in the Fourth Gospel. At most its existence may be suggested in such statements as "all things were made by him" (1:3) and "the word became flesh." There is little question, however, that the existence and nature of such opposition is more certain and more clearly defined in the letters, especially 1 John. The Gospel and Epistles, and even the Book of Revelation (chapters 2 and 3), certainly attest the existence of a form of early Christianity in which the tradition and memory of Jesus was held in tension with Spirit inspiration and, presumably, prophecy. The volatile nature of such Christianity is not difficult to imagine, and that nature is what we see reflected in the Johannine writings. Such a Christianity stood in danger of losing contact with its traditional heritage, and therefore with Jesus. Both the Gospel and 1 John are concerned with the continuing relationship between Jesus and his community. In 1 John a threat to that relationship is clearly perceived and opposed.

CHAPTER SIX

THE JOHANNINE PERSPECTIVES: A SUMMARY

John sets Jesus Christ in three different, but related, hermeneutical frames. He is, first of all, the only Son of God, the Word through whom the worlds were made, the light of all men. Thus the glory that manifests itself in his word and works is more than the anticipation of eschatological glory, as, for example, are Jesus' demon exorcisms in the synoptic Gospels, which anticipate the eschatological kingdom of God (Matt. 12:28). John intends his readers to understand the cosmic significance of Jesus. His pre-existent glory, his being with the Father before the foundation of the world (17:5, 24), his role in creation (1:1ff.), his being sent by God (3:16), all indicate something of the significance, dignity, and meaning of Jesus. He is the definitive, exhaustive, and final revelation of God in and to this world. As such he is, and must be, present and active in the creation of this world.

One would be mistaken to imagine that this kind of language is taken seriously by John only as a mythical or symbolic way of saying something about Jesus that could as easily be said in other, more abstract or philosophical terms. Whether John means his language about pre-existence to be taken literally, or whether and how he imagines Jesus' pre-existent dwelling with God are questions that admit of no certain or definitive answers. Yet it is safe to assume that John writes as he does, and has Jesus speak as he does, because he believes such language and imagery are best suited to convey the reality of God's revelation in Jesus. We can easily imagine John's putting some distance between himself and his linguistic and conceptual tools. His theological depth and perceptivity suggest that his use of mythical language and miracle tradition is qualified by a theological subtlety which sees their problems and limitations. But because we find this so conceivable does not mean that we have the right to assume that he consciously and deliberately made such a move. As much sophistication as John may manifest, he is nevertheless also the child and creature of a culture and of religious and intellectual traditions distinctly different from our own. It may be that we can legitimately distinguish between John's fundamental theological intent on the one hand and his possibilities for expressing that intent on the other. But we may not as a matter of course impute to him the distinctions that our intellectual perspective allows us to draw.

John tells us that Jesus lived with the Father before the creation of the world, that all things were made through him, that he was sent into the world when it became alienated from God and darkened to reveal God's truth and rekindle the light of the knowledge of God among men, and that having been judged and crucified by the rulers of this world he has now returned to God, whence his Spirit is given to encourage, inspire, and instruct his own, his disciples, whom the world also hates. Not surprisingly many Johannine scholars have seen in this scenario affinities with Gnosticism. (As we have seen, 1 John apparently struggles against the kind of docetic Christology that was typical of Gnosticism.) That there was some relationship is altogether probable. How to define it, or in what direction it moves, are matters that presently divide the most learned opinions. Whether Gnostic or not, John sees in Jesus and bears testimony to a revelation of God so crucial, decisive, and epoch-making that it must be described in the most far-reaching cosmic terms.

This revelation is also historical; otherwise it would scarcely be revelation. It occurs in history and in a personal history. The Gospel of John is not the best place to start in search of the historical Jesus. Probably the Gospel does not strongly emphasize the humanity of Jesus because in the face of the rejection of his divine commission his revelatory role—that is, his unity with God —requires emphasis. Later on, in a Christian context, 1 John found it necessary to underscore the human dimension against those who seemed to reject it. John is, however, as fully committed as any of the canonical Evangelists to the proposition that Jesus was a historical figure whose character and deeds were of such a nature as to warrant, if not prove, the claims made for him. But the Jews, or the world, do not reject Jesus and the revelation of God in him simply because they cannot tolerate and accept the claim that God reveals himself in one who is but a human being. Rather, despite Jesus' salvific deeds and words, or even because of them, they reject, persecute, and crucify him. Because he claims and acts out the role of the Messiah, the world rises up to strike him down. Or so John portrays it.

Did things actually happen just so? The synoptic Gospels afford ample ground for questioning whether they actually did. Jesus was certainly known as an exorcist (a role in which John does not portray him) and miracle worker; but he did not go about proclaiming himself as Messiah, whatever he may have thought about his role, much less arguing at length with his opponents. Moreover, the synoptics are probably right in portraying Jesus as unwilling to work miracles as signs, whereas in John he takes the initiative in doing just that. Certainly Jesus provoked opposition in some Jewish circles, but he did not see himself and his disciples arrayed over against Judaism as if they were not themselves Jews. In this respect also John's representation seems not to be historical.

What do we mean by historical? In this context the presumed meaning is "accurately representing the historical figure of Jesus in his relationship with his contemporaries." We have, however, already seen that such a representation of Jesus would have been regarded by John as a distortion and truncation of his reality, even of his historic reality. In his view the historical reality of Jesus extends from the time of his death on into the life and struggles of this community.[35] In the Spirit (or Paraclete) Jesus' presence continues among his disciples, the church. For John, Jesus' ministry had at least two dimensions.

So the Johannine controversies between Jesus and the Jews are not historical in the sense that they are reports of what went on between Jesus and the people he encountered in his ministry in or about A.D. 30 in Galilee and Judea. They may, however, be historical in another sense. That is, they portray the tension, struggle, and polemics between Jesus' Jewish followers and those who did not share their beliefs about him. Doubtless this struggle developed over a period of several decades. We see the struggle dramatized in chapters 5 and 9. Almost certainly the form in which it lies before us in the present Gospel dates from the period after the Jewish War (A.D. 66–70), and the Gospel itself from the final decade of the first century. Yet there is a certain continuity between the historical ministry of Jesus with struggles and conflicts ending in his death and the struggles and conflicts of the church of his followers. Jesus' own actions and his preaching of the near advent of the kingdom or rule of God raised acute questions about his intention, mission, and role. These questions became more narrowly focused as the post-resurrection church announced him to be the Messiah or messiah-designate and awaited his return as Son of man at the imminent end of this age. Their convictions about Jesus and the significance of his coming precipitated increasing conflict with other Jews, which are reflected in the synoptic tradition (e.g., Mark 2:1—3:6) or Gospels (cf. Matthew 23). In the Johannine community conflict seems to have focused rather narrowly upon the claims made for Jesus concerning his unique relationship to God (5:18). But in either case the role of Jesus stood at the center of attention and controversy. According to John, the history of Jesus and his Jewish compatriots includes the post-resurrection controversies over who he is which issue in the formation of a separate religious confession and community around him. Because John sees this controversy as being of a piece with Jesus' ministry, he can portray Jesus as the principal protagonist of his own cause in arguing that he is the Christ, the Son of God. So John presents Jesus as historic in this dual sense, that is, in his own time and in the subsequent controversies about him.

But for the Evangelist Jesus is also a present reality, that is, contemporary and present with the church of his followers. Accordingly, in addressing his disciples in the farewell discourses and elsewhere he also addresses his Christian contemporaries and the problems and issues faced by the church. There is in the discourses a subtle duality of focus. On the one hand, the disciples while looking to Jesus as Lord still reflect an ignorance about him that corresponds with their pre-resurrection perspective. Yet in his final prayer Jesus speaks of them as possessing Christian knowledge to which they could scarcely as yet have attained. At the same time Jesus speaks in these discourses in terms which, while they cannot be fully comprehended by the disciples at that point in time, are relevant and appropriate to the post-resurrection church for which John writes. At the turn of the century the problems of eschatology (the nonoccurrence of the expected parousia), the transmission and preservation of the traditional image of Jesus versus the role of the Spirit, and the hostility of the world called for a statement of the gospel and a reassertion of its indispensable basis in, and determination by, Jesus. In view of that situation, and drawing upon the memory and traditions of his community, the Evangelist composed the Gospel of John. Thus he sought to assert the bond between the community of disciples and Jesus. As we have just seen, the author of 1 John under different circumstances wrote to secure that same goal.

INTERPRETATION

Interpretation may go on at several levels, and in the Christian tradition should and must do so. In Part II the focus was on specific Johannine texts with a view to discovering the meaning of those texts in light of their historical contexts, references, and connections. Some important threads were exposed and teased out, so to speak. Some things we now understand much better.

In Part III we attempt to tie threads together and see how they look. First, we give an interpretation of the Fourth Gospel as a historical document, asking about its testimony to Jesus and about its testimony to the church and wider religious, cultural and social setting in which it was composed. We have some direct knowledge of this setting from the Johannine letters. Because John has been read for millenia by Christians who have known little or nothing of these historical circumstances, we turn next to an exploration of how the Gospel of John may be read on its own terms. Such an analysis should shed light on, perhaps confirm (or disconfirm), aspects of the historical interpretation.

Finally, we take note of the fact that the Gospel of John is set in the context of the NT canon. It is read alongside twenty-six other books or writings, and particularly alongside three other Gospels, which, as we have seen, differ rather significantly from it. How does this state of affairs affect the understanding of the Fourth Gospel? What does it imply for the interpretation of the Fourth Gospel as a canonical document? Is the Jesus of the Fourth Gospel to be isolated from the rather different presentation of Jesus in the other Gospels? Or, are John and the synoptics to be allowed to shed light on one another? These are questions in need of further and fuller consideration.

CHAPTER SEVEN

INTERPRETING THE HISTORICAL ORIGINS OF THE FOURTH GOSPEL

Roots in the Ministry of Jesus

As we have already observed, John intends to speak of Jesus, and he does so by narrating his ministry, death, and resurrection. It may seem to us that in recounting the story of Jesus he only did the obvious thing. But what appears obvious to us may have seemed less so to John or his contemporaries. The form of the synoptic Gospels exercised at most a general influence upon him, if he knew one or more of them at all. His Gospel differs in many and unaccountable ways from the others, despite some significant similarities. Furthermore, others who undertook to write about Jesus, in John's time and in the century thereafter, sometimes took entirely different paths and used other literary forms. Thus the so-called Gospel of Truth (ca. 150) is a theological meditation on the gospel as understood by Valentinian Gnostics. The Gospel of Thomas (also ca. 150) is a collection of Jesus' sayings similar to the earlier, and still hypothetical, Q source of Matthew and Luke. Both of these Gospels were, of course, adjudged heterodox by the later church. But within the canon also there are interesting departures from, or alternatives, to, the gospel form.

It never occurred to Paul to write a gospel; he was too busy writing letters in order to deal directly with the affairs of the churches which he had founded. Probably he also did not have immediate and direct access to the Jesus tradition in sufficient quantity to justify such an undertaking had it occurred to him as a possibility. The epistolary form then acquired great favor in earlier Christianity, probably through Paul's influence, even when it was not actually necessary or called for. For example, the author of Hebrews writes in semi-epistolary form what amounts to a theological treatise (cf. also 1 John, 1 Peter, James). In doing so he manifests a conception of Jesus' earthly ministry and some knowledge of specific traditions about him (e.g., Gethsemane, Heb. 5:7; location of Golgotha, 13:12). It is by no means clear, however, that the author knew any gospel, and in any event he does not set about to write one.

John the author of Revelation, writing near the end of the first century, delivers words of the heavenly Christ to the Church on earth (especially chaps. 1—3; also 22) and allows us to glimpse a heavenly scenario in which Christ plays a central role. Obviously, the material of Revelation is not suitable for a gospel-like narrative of Jesus' ministry. (It may nevertheless be the case that some traditional words of the earthly Jesus are buried in the discourses of

Revelation, while in all probability Spirit-inspired, prophetically delivered words of the heavenly Lord are found in the canonical Gospels.) If John of Patmos could have written a gospel-like narrative, he obviously did not choose to do so, because his interests led him in another direction. He too wants to speak of Jesus, but not of the earthly, historical figure.

The implications of these diverse observations for the question of the character and form of the Fourth Gospel are clear enough. The author was not bound to produce a narrative of Jesus' ministry leading up to his death. The synoptic Gospels, if they were known to him, could have suggested the genre he adopted, but obviously did not exercise a determinative influence over him. Other literary forms or models were available to him, as both the non-canonical "gospels" and other canonical documents show. John therefore chose to write a gospel and this choice is significant. Despite his weighty theological, polemical, and churchly interests, he elected to say what he thought most important by rehearsing the words, deeds, death, and resurrection of Jesus, and this is a fact of no small consequence for understanding this document. That John, his community and tradition, placed a high value on the historical, event-character of Jesus' ministry is a legitimate inference from the literary form that he chose. It is significant that his magnum opus is not a letter, a revelation discourse, or an apocalypse. Moreover, the importance of what has happened, and the existence of witnesses to it, is repeatedly and explicitly underlined in the Gospel (1:14; 15:27; 19:35; 21:24; cf. 1 John 1:1–4). Whatever may be said about the value of the Fourth Gospel in coming to an understanding of the historical Jesus, there can be no doubt that the Gospel was written in order to contribute to such an understanding.[36] In fact, one may go so far as to say that the Gospel was written to define, under a specific set of circumstances, the proper understanding of Jesus. Naturally, to say this is not to endorse the Gospel as historical according to generally accepted, modern standards of historicity or historical investigation. John's understanding of Jesus, along with his understanding of history, is distinctive, if not unique.

Yet in any consideration of the Gospel of John the historical dimension must be kept in view. To do otherwise would be unfair to the ancient author. John indicates he is describing Jesus, a figure of the past, and acknowledges that the trustworthiness of the basis of that description is important. The Gospel also encompasses considerable traditional material. This is particularly the case in the passion and other narratives, although traditional material is not absent from the sayings of Jesus (e.g., 12:25–26; cf. Mark 8:35 parr.; Matt. 10:39; Luke 9:24; 14:26). Perhaps most important John shows an awareness of the existence of what we may accurately call "the historical problem" that is unmatched in other Gospels. His clear recognition of a decisive advantage of perspective available to the post-resurrection church, although not to the disciples of Jesus during his earthly ministry, is repeatedly attested in the farewell discourses, as well as at other points in the Gospel (2:17, 22; 7:39; 12:16).

We are entitled to believe that if John effected a transformation of the Jesus tradition he received, or conveyed to his readers a transformed tradition, he was not altogether innocent of what he was doing. The Fourth Gospel is certainly no objective, disinterested, chronicle of Jesus' ministry. Yet it points continuously to that ministry and is, in some sense, rooted in it.

The Question of Authorship

In view of the explicit interest in the historical question manifest in the Fourth Gospel, as well as the several apparent references to an apostolic eyewitness authority standing behind the Gospel as guarantor and, indeed, author, it is not surprising that the tradition that John the Apostle wrote the Fourth Gospel took hold and became generally accepted in the latter part of the second century. In all probability this attribution of the Gospel to John and the acknowledgment of apostolic authorship by the church had much to do with the acceptance of the Gospel into the canon. By the nineteenth century when critical questions were raised about this attribution it had become a generally held assumption among Christians and was widely regarded as an important, even indispensable, fundament of Christian faith. Criticism of the now orthodox view was tantamount to heresy, and the Roman Catholic church, through the decrees of the Biblical Commission, specifically enjoined its biblical scholars to affirm Johannine authorship of the Fourth Gospel.[37] Traditional Protestant opinion was of the same order.

Thus the Evangelist John was identified with the Son of Zebedee, the brother of James, and was taken to be the author of the Epistles of John and the Book of Revelation as well as the Fourth Gospel. John the son of Zebedee is mentioned rather frequently in the synoptic Gospels. With James he was called by Jesus from his occupation as a fisherman (Mark 1:19). These two brothers, called "Sons of Thunder" (Mark 3:18), with Simon, and sometimes his brother Andrew, formed the inner circle of Jesus' disciples according to the synoptics. Needless to say, John appears in all four canonical lists of the Twelve. In the Gospels' lists his name appears after James' (Matt. 10:2; Mark 3:17; Luke 6:14), but in Acts 1:13 John appears second, after Peter only. This promotion fits the Acts portrayal, where in the early chapters John accompanies Peter in several important scenes (e.g., 3:1, 4, 11; 8:14). John was not an unimportant figure. But, interestingly enough, exactly those episodes in which John appears in the synoptic accounts are missing from the Fourth Gospel, where the sons of Zebedee are mentioned only once, in the appendix (21:2), and not by name.

Like the other Gospels, the Fourth Gospel is anonymous, although at the end (21:24) it is apparently ascribed to the so-called Beloved Disciple, who appears only in the final scenes in Jerusalem. Except for one episode at the cross (19:25–27), he always appears together with Peter (as John appears with Peter in Acts). Since the end of the second century Christian tradition has unanimously identified this disciple with John the son of Zebedee, but that identification is not made within the Gospel itself, or the NT generally.

We confront a strange and unexplained phenomenon. Until near the end of the second century the authorship of the Fourth Gospel seems to have been a mystery. Where it was apparently known its author was not named. From the beginning of the third century onward, however, almost everyone agrees that it is the work of the disciple John, who composed it in Ephesus, after he had read the other Gospels, perhaps late in his life. In the late second century Irenaeus traced the Johannine tradition to Bishops Papias and Polycarp, who lived near Ephesus in the mid-second century (Eusebius, *Ecclesiastical History* 3.39.1–7; 4.14.3–8), but his testimony may have been inaccurate, as Eusebius himself suggested.

The Gospel of John was obviously known in some Christian circles through much of the second century. We find traces of it, perhaps in Ignatius (ca. 115–120) and almost certainly in Justin Martyr (ca. 140–160). Yet it was particularly popular among Gnostics and others later rejected as heretics. Certain orthodox churchmen (e.g., Gaius of Rome) objected to it, pointing out its apparently irreconcilable differences from the synoptics. While such differences are significant, the real motivation was probably its heretical associations. Apparently the Fourth Gospel was not generally regarded as an apostolic writing by many Christians until a later period. Ultimately, the Gospel, the Johannine Epistles, and Revelation were all acknowledged as apostolic, and as such were regarded as the work of the Galilean John, the brother of James and son of Zebedee. Exactly how this came about is unclear; the prevailing consensus begins to take shape at the end of the second century but presents problems.

For example, the traditional view that John lived to a ripe old age in Ephesus lacks attestation at a critical point. When Bishop Ignatius of Antioch wrote to the church in Ephesus in the second decade of the first century, he made much of Paul's Ephesian residence, but did not mention John at all. (Ignatius may allude to the Fourth Gospel, but does not cite it.) An Ephesian residence of John, but not the writing of a Gospel, is mentioned in the Leucian Acts of John. On the other hand, that document possibly reflects knowledge of the Gospel. Jesus' prediction of Mark 10:39 suggests that both James and John will be martyred. We know that James was killed by Herod Agrippa in Jerusalem in the early 40s. A martyrology dating from several centuries later supports the possibility that John also died. Nevertheless, John seems to have been alive and well in Jerusalem in the later years of the same decade (cf. Gal. 2:9). Evidently he did not die with James. However that may be, a number of difficulties stand in the way of tracing later church tradition about John the Evangelist back to the beginning of the second century.

If the Gospel had been known or acknowledged in the second-century church as the work of John, or of any apostle, its relative disuse among the orthodox in the second century and the outright opposition to it in some circles would be difficult to explain. Probably the almost simultaneous ascription of the Gospel to John and the wide acceptance and citation of it in the church were not unrelated. Naturally, this does not prove that the ascription was incorrect, but with the other evidence we have mentioned it does constitute a strong case against acceptance of the traditional view of authorship. Thus in recent years exegesis has as a rule not proceeded on the assumption of Johannine authorship, even when that tradition has not been explicitly rejected. While some conservative Christians have regarded this turn of events as possibly leading to disaster for orthodox Christian faith, an even broader spectrum of theological opinion, Catholic and Protestant, has come to terms with it.

The Johannine Circle or School

If the question of authorship seems less crucial than it once did, an important reason has been the well-founded and growing suspicion that the Gospel in the form in which we now have it is the product of more than one hand. Efforts to analyze the Fourth Gospel into its components have multiplied since the beginning of the century, culminating in the ingeniously complex literary theory of Rudolf Bultmann, who in his justly famous commentary on John distributed the entire Gospel among several sources, an author, and a later redactor.[38] Bultmann's analysis attracted few scholars who could accept it in detail, but suggested something significant about the complexity of the process that produced the Gospel, and about its constituent parts.

The kinds of phenomena which Bultmann described almost wholly in terms of literary analysis may be accorded a somewhat greater plausibility when set in a social context, that is, a Johannine school, church, or community. Of course, such a context is suggested by considerations other than the necessity of saving the credibility of a kind of literary analysis. There are, in fact, good reasons for thinking that John emerged from a school or circles of early Christianity in which distinct traditions and a characteristic perspective on the gospel were preserved and fostered.

As we have already observed, the Johannine Epistles presuppose a circle of communities or churches in which a particular understanding of the gospel flourished. The author of the letters understands himself to be responsible for the doctrine and welfare of those churches. Although with some reason it was long assumed that the letters and Gospel were the work of a single author, there are certain differences of style and theological expression that make it difficult to ascribe them all to the same hand.[39] If they are, in fact, from two or more authors, they attest the existence of a Johannine sphere of influence in which a similar theological language and a common homiletical style were current.

Various aspects of the Gospel also point in the same direction. The statements of 21:23–24 about the death of the Beloved Disciple and the authorship of the Gospel are richly suggestive of a constituency in which the Gospel would be read. In this regard the desire to correct a misunderstanding of Jesus' word about the Beloved Disciple is particularly significant. Why was it necessary to set aside a rumor concerning what Jesus had said about him? Was he a widely acknowledged leader among the anticipated readers of the Gospel? His privileged position—from the Last Supper onward he is always close to Jesus—would seem to suggest this. Is there some historical reason why he is portrayed in a sort of rivalry with Peter, the widely acknowledged leader among the early Christians, in which Peter comes off second best? Yet in chapter 21 we find an explicit interest in the reinstatement of Peter. Probably the Beloved Disciple, whose historical identity is irrecoverable, is or symbolizes the authoritative figure in the Johannine community.[40] By the same token, Peter himself is certainly an authoritative figure in the church, perhaps in rival but not hostile circles.

When one turns to the substance of the Gospel itself further interesting questions and possibilities present themselves. What is the proximate origin of the narrative and discourse materials, that is, where did the Evangelist himself obtain them? If he was not an eyewitness, the most probable alternatives are either that he composed them himself *de novo* or that he relied on some earlier tradition, that is, they were mediated (whether or not in written form is another question) to him through a social process, a community of Christians to which he or they—more likely both—belonged.

The miracle and passion narratives especially suggest this. The miracle stories, when considered apart from the discourses and debates which accompany them, are not unlike the miracle stories of the synoptics in form and probable function. (They may differ somewhat insofar as Jesus, in typically Johannine fashion, tends to take initiatives which accentuate his miraculous powers.) Of course, some of them are obviously parallels of the synoptic stories. Nevertheless, their very existence and form attest the existence of a community in which they were preserved, told, and retold. The passion narrative is by far the richest and longest continuous source of Johannine parallels with the synoptics. If John's passion narrative is not actually dependent upon one or more of them, and the evidence for dependence is not compelling, we ought nevertheless consider the Johannine account, or whatever source may underlie it, as the product of a community which shared some of the same traditions as Mark and the other synoptics. The Johannine passion narrative presumably also answered the needs of the community to explain and justify theologically the crucial events leading up to and including Jesus' death. The parallels with the synoptics (as well as certain differences), the use of OT quotations, the solemn assertion of the truth of the report and reliability of the eyewitness (19:35) all point in this direction. In all probability the strong Jewish opposition to Jesus in the passion, especially the trial, scenes reflects an increasing

Jewish-Christian hostility in the milieu in which the Gospel was written. The same sort of hostility seems to be the background of the vigorously polemical reactions of the crowds and especially the Jews to the signs of Jesus which appear in the conversations and debates following his deeds.

We have already noted the significance of the way the Jews, and often the Pharisees specifically, are portrayed as the opponents of Jesus and have suggested that this perspective mirrors the situation of a Christian community in conflict with the synagogue (pp. 38–51 above). The specter of excommunication from the synagogue in all probability takes us back to a period in which Christians, that is, Jews who confessed Jesus to be the Messiah, felt themselves threatened with expulsion from the synagogue if they persisted in their confession. Probably this threat arose only after the Roman War (ended A.D. 70) and the retrenchment of Judaism and its reconstitution under Pharisaic dominance at the Council of Jamnia (Yavneh) under the leadership of Rabbis Yohanan ben Zakkai and Gamaliel. If the threat of expulsion was related to the "Twelfth Benediction," which pronounces a malediction upon *minim* and Nazarenes, then the situation the Gospel presupposes can have existed no earlier than the 80s.[41]

By the time our Gospel was written, however, the Johannine Christians already stood outside the synagogue. The statements about the threat of being cast out of the synagogue already suggest this (9:22; 12:42; 16:2). That is, what is portrayed as a threat in the time of Jesus is, by inference, to be viewed as an accomplished fact among Christians (cf. 16:2). Moreover, the references to Jesus' opponents and to unbelievers as "the Jews" is otherwise difficult to comprehend. Yet the memory of the break and the resulting trauma seem very much alive, as the vehemence of the polemic on both sides—Jesus' (i.e., his disciples') and the Jews—suggests. The date of composition usually proposed, that is, between 90 and 100, accommodates this course of events rather well.[42] It is late enough to allow for a Jewish retrenchment and a separation of Christians from the synagogue following the disaster of the Roman war, but early enough to account for why the pain and sharp hostility accompanying the rupture are still very much alive. That the conversations and debates of the Fourth Gospel are suffused with hostility between Jesus and, by clear implication, his followers and the Jews is itself indicative of the relations and rivalry between the two religious communities. Perhaps something of the ingredients and course of their controversy can be inferred from the content of the Gospel itself.

For example, except for the encounters with Nicodemus and the Samaritan woman, the account of the *deeds* of Jesus in his public ministry is largely confined to miracles. Even these encounters invoke or are closely related to Jesus' miracle-working activity. Nicodemus is attracted to Jesus because of his signs (3:2). The Samaritan woman acknowledges the messiahship of Jesus because of his supernatural knowledge of her past (4:29–30). Moreover, the narration of a miracle is the occasion for and is typically followed by a discussion with the Jews about the legitimacy and meaning of the miracle. The discussions take on an increasingly hostile tone as they develop, with claims being made for Jesus which are denied by the Jews. Although the miraculous signs of Jesus do not remain continuously in the forefront of discussion, there is recurring reference to them. It may well be that the role of the signs in the Gospel debates about Jesus' identity is indicative of the role played by miracles in the discussions between Christians and Jews which are an important part of the background of this Gospel. The miracle story, understood by Jesus' disciples and presumably by the Johannine church as a sign, serves the progress of the narrative by getting things going between Jesus and his interlocutors (who, of course, become his opponents and accusers). It is not unreasonable to suppose that historically the miracle stories actually functioned in that way, that is, as a sort of catalyst in actual discussions between Jews and Christians (i.e., Jews who believed in Jesus) about Jesus. If so, we must suppose that these Christians put Jesus' miracles forward as signs of who he was. They were at the least talking points, at most putative proofs, in such discussions.[43]

According to the dominant Jewish messianic expectations of the time, miracle-working may not have been a function, at least not an important function, of the Davidic Messiah. Nevertheless, Jesus was known among his disciples and others as a miracle worker, and the performance of mighty works as proof of divine commission or sanction was deeply imbedded in the Jewish and biblical tradition, as the signs of Moses before Pharaoh certainly prove. (In fact, there are some remarkable affinities between the Mosaic signs and the Johannine Jesus' signs.) As the discussions of the signs in the Gospel progress and hostility mounts a sharp sunderance between those who believe in Jesus and those who do not develops. Quite possibly this development closely parallels actual relations between Jews and Christians in the period before, and leading up to, the composition of the Gospel. The Johannine dualism of light and darkness, truth and lie, above and below, God and Satan comes into play in order to comprehend the total antinomy and contradiction that exists between Jesus and his followers and those who reject him (see chap. 8 especially). This dualism has sometimes, and with good reason, been described either as ethical or ontological, with some debate over which of these dimensions is dominant. However that may be, the dualism is almost certainly socially conditioned. That is, it mirrors the disjuncture and hostility that has developed between the now separate Jewish and Christian communities.[44]

This hostility also figures in John's presentation of the trial and death of Jesus. After chapter 12 Jesus no longer confronts the Jews directly, except for the brief hearing before Annas after his arrest (18:19–24), in which the characteristic themes of Jesus' controversies with the Jews do not appear. The chief trial scene is before Pilate (18:8—19:15) and a long interrogation and conversation between Jesus and Pilate which has no real synoptic counterpart is recounted. In this scene a number of Johannine theological points are made as the interrogation proceeds. The main question, found also in the synoptics, is put forward by Pilate: "Are you the king of the Jews?" (18:33). This question receives a typically Johannine answer: "My kingdom is not of this world" (18:36). Pilate attempts for a while to play the role of mediator between Jesus and the Jews, but they are obdurate, and he finally succumbs to their thinly veiled threat to portray him as an enemy of Caesar if he releases Jesus (19:12). Even then Pilate does not order Jesus' crucifixion but appears to accede to the Jews' condemnation of him, turning him over to them to be crucified (19:15–16). Mark 15:15 says simply that Pilate "handed Jesus over," apparently to the Roman soldiers who then proceed to crucify him (cf. 15:16ff.). John, however, reports that Pilate handed Jesus over "to them" (i.e., the Jews). Whether by coincidence or not, John avoids saying explicitly that the soldiers crucified Jesus (19:17). The unknowing reader might think the Jewish authorities did it, even though in 18:31 they admit they do not have the *jus gladii* (the power to execute). The scene before Pilate thus becomes a means whereby the culmination of Jewish hostility to Jesus is displayed and underscored, although Jesus does not there confront his opponents directly.

The historical truth of these narratives is less our concern than the historical setting which gave them their present shape and definition. Suffice it to say that whatever role Jewish authorities or people played in the trial and execution of Jesus has been overemphasized and exaggerated in the Fourth Gospel. Prominent among the factors betrayed in all these narratives and the conversations based upon them is surely the sect-type consciousness which has developed within the Johannine Christian circle in its struggle with Judaism and has become so integral a part of its thinking and lifestyle, as well as self-consciousness. Johannine Christianity shares with early Christianity generally a sense of alienation, or separateness, from the world. More strongly than other branches of the early church, however, John's community defines itself over against that hostile world. They have seen and heard the incarnate Word from the Father above and walk by his light into eternal life. The world may have also seen and heard, but it has not truly perceived him, and in rejecting him it condemns itself and sinks further into darkness toward the death which is its destiny. In some such terms the Johannine community defines itself over against the world.

Does it also define itself over against the rest of Christendom? Yes and no. There is little unambiguous evidence that the Gospel of John understands the gospel of its community as uniquely true as compared to other versions which are false. The view that John intends explicitly to reject the forms of Christianity found in the synoptic tradition is, as we have noted, scarcely tenable. Considerably more probable is the view that Johannine Christianity represents the development of an archaic, spirit-inspired form of Christianity which relied for its leadership and authority upon persons chosen informally for their charismatic qualities or prophetic gifts.[45] Over against such Christianity is placed the developing orthodox church represented in the Fourth Gospel by Peter. Certainly Peter and the Beloved Disciple appear as rivals in the Fourth Gospel, with the Beloved Disciple consistently winning out. But Peter is not disparaged or dismissed. Indeed, in the end he is rehabilitated. John is not simply antithetical to other forms of early Christianity. Yet its distinctive spiritual character is clear, as is the central importance of the distinctive figure of the Beloved Disciple. In fact, that disciple and the Paraclete seem to play analogous roles, linking the Johannine community to Jesus. In 1 John (4:1–3) the claim of spiritual authority has begun to present problems, as it almost inevitably would. Obviously credal and official authority must assert itself.

How this assertion of authority is occurring is hard to know with respect to the individuals named in the letters. For example, it is really impossible to know for sure how the Elder, the author of 3 John, stands in relation to his antagonist Diotrephes (v. 9). The view that the Elder struggles against an aspirant to the rank or status and powers of the episcopal office is plausible. Yet it can also be argued that the Elder (and author) is really the one wielding, or attempting to wield, such power in the church and that Diotrephes refuses to accede to his authority or aspires to the same office! However that may be, it is nonetheless clear that the Johannine Christian community is not able to live in complete tranquility. Certainly 1 John reflects a struggle over doctrine, as does 2 John. Has Jesus Christ really come in the flesh? 3 John was written because of an inner church struggle of a serious sort. Possibly these conflicts have also found some subtler expression within the Gospel. We should not think of Johannine Christianity as a monolithic doctrinal or organizational unity. Rather it is a community of common origin, language or rhetoric, and theological interests which includes, or has at its circumference, considerable theological diversity. There is a question as to how the typically Johannine insights will be developed. Probably both Diotrephes and the Elder, as well as both the author of 1 John and those who deny the fleshly reality of Jesus, were in a real sense Johannine Christians.[46]

It has become commonplace to refer to the sphere of Johannine influence within early Christianity as the Johannine school. That usage is certainly justifiable in that "school" in English may refer to "a group of persons . . . sharing certain principles, canons, precepts, or a body of opinion or practice."[47] Certainly Johannine Christianity constitutes a school in this sense. The question of whether it may be considered a school in a narrower and historically specifiable sense is, however, a significant one. Allusions to a Johannine school in antiquity, the similarity of language, rhetoric, and theology between the Gospel and letters, and the evidence for midrashic development of OT quotations and traditions within the Gospel all make the matter seem worth pursuing.

A recent investigation reveals that ancient schools generally, whether Jewish or Hellenistic, shared the following characteristics: "1) They were groups of disciples which usually emphasized *philia* and *koinonia*; 2) they gathered around, and traced their origins to a founder whom they regarded as an exemplary wise, or good (virtuous) man; 3) they valued the teachings of their founder and the traditions about him; 4) members of the schools were disciples or students of the founder; 5) teaching, learning, studying, and writing were common activities; 6) most schools observed communal meals, often in memory of their founders; 7) they had rules or practices regarding admission and retention of membership, and advancement within the membership; 8) they often maintained some degree of distance or withdrawal from the rest of society; and 9) they developed organizational means of insuring their perpetuity."[48] Obviously, the Christian movement or the church itself corresponds fairly closely to most of these specifications. Yet it very quickly spread and was scattered across the Greco-Roman world; at the same time schism and diversity developed within it. Phenomenologically, the Johannine circle presents a much more compact entity for close scrutiny and analysis. Within it the figure of the Beloved Disciple in the Gospel or the Elder in the letters functions for the school as a means of mediating the tradition of the community and the authority of Jesus. This tradition and authority is, or course, subject to the work of the Spirit, who represents the reality and revelation of Jesus to the community. While the Johannine circle within the church may not have possessed a sect-type consciousness vis-à-vis other churches or Christians, it stood over against the world and Judaism as a distinct form of Christianity with a certain internal cohesiveness, despite the threat and even the actuality of schism. While the community as a whole may not have thought of itself as a school, it possessed within itself, and particularly in its interest in preserving and transmitting the revelation (or teaching) with which it had been entrusted, certain pronounced scholastic functions and techniques.

To summarize, the Gospel of John has historic roots, in interest and tradition, in the ministry of Jesus. It describes Jesus' ministry of miracles (signs), teaching, controversy, arrest, trial, and death, and narrates the whole from the perspective of faith in his resurrection. Although it was not written by John, the son of Zebedee, it looks to a tradition and memory of Jesus' ministry and words, preserved at first within the synagogue. After the Jewish-Roman war and the retrenchment of the Jewish community along Pharisaic lines, the position of Jesus' adherents within the synagogue became intolerable and a separation took place. Because of the trauma of the rupture, the Johannine Christian community defined and understood itself as the obverse of the synagogue and saw in the latter the enemy par excellence. But the hostility to the synagogue was matched by the rejection of the world generally, and the community came to regard the Jewish opposition as archetypical of this rejection. The community's faith and hope are reflected in the Johannine letters, but they found definitive expression in the Gospel. Standing over against the world the Johannine Christians sought to stabilize themselves and secure their relationship to the originating events of Jesus' ministry. Thus certain crucial functions within the community were organized along lines analogous to ancient schools. Over and beyond the factors already mentioned in this chapter, several theological problems distinctive of, and arising from, the situation of these Christians in their life together and in their relation to the world were causative and formative forces in the origins and composition of the Gospel. To these we shall now turn.

CHAPTER EIGHT

THEOLOGICAL FACTORS INFLUENCING THE DEVELOPMENT OF JOHANNINE THOUGHT

Of the factors influencing the development of Johannine theology, the Evangelist's interest in rooting his Gospel in the history and tradition of Jesus and the continuing dialogue and conflict with Judaism have already been discussed. We have also taken note of the world's general hostility to Christianity, which is reflected in the Gospel and epitomized in "the Jews." That John's Gospel, and Johannine Christianity generally, bear witness to problems and conflicts in the development of church organization and doctrine has also become clear.

Johannine and Other Forms of Christianity

The extent to which Johannine Christianity was in contact with other forms of Christianity represented in the NT is a good question, but perhaps admits of no definitive resolution. Certainly critical opinion has now shifted away from the once widely held assumption that the fourth Evangelist knew both Paul's letters[49] and the synoptic Gospels. The relation of John to the synoptics has been the subject of considerable critical investigation, which has moved in the direction of denying or at least calling into question the earlier view that John knew, used, and deliberately altered or supplemented the synoptics.[50] Whether or not it is still held that John knew the synoptics at all, dependence on them is generally denied or affirmed with qualification. For most exegetes neither one nor all of the synoptics is a base line from which Johannine interpretation must begin. Nevertheless, the many points of contact between the Fourth Gospel and the synoptic tradition are undeniable. John may not have known the synoptic Gospels, but he at least knew and used traditional narratives to which the synoptic Evangelists also had access. The Fourth Gospel represents a distinct, relatively independent, but by no means isolated form of early Christianity.

What is said of the relation of John's Gospel to the synoptics may also be said of its relationship to Paul, although the question of a possible connection between John and Paul has not in recent years been the subject of very active investigation. John embodies certain important theological themes or emphases in common with Paul, but cannot be viewed as a development of, or as the basis of, Pauline theology. There are some passages in John's Gospel which may reflect Pauline influence (e.g., 1:17; 8:30–37), but by and large

John seems to address a different situation and set of problems. For example, although John, with Paul, underscores repeatedly the importance of faith in Jesus, he does not set faith over against works of the law as alternative means of justification. The Jewish law can simply be referred to as "your law" (10:34; cf. 7:51, where Nicodemus refers to "our law"), as if it were a thing with which Christians were no longer concerned. The world is indeed regarded as enslaved by sin, but the role of the law in accentuating this situation is not considered. Not the law, but the doctrine of Christ, is the center of controversy. Thus, in some ways John seems further removed from the Jewish roots of Christianity than Paul. While the precise relationship between Johannine and Pauline forms of Christianity awaits futher definition, one thing can be said with confidence: the exegesis of the Gospel of John or of Johannine texts cannot proceed on Pauline premises or on the assumption that John was familiar with and presupposed the Pauline letters and theology.

John a Missionary Gospel?

The heavy emphasis upon the necessity of belief in Jesus Christ, including the final statement of 20:30–31, has long led interpreters to see in John a missionary emphasis if not a missionary gospel. It has frequently been thought that John was written primarily to induce and encourage belief, that is, Christian faith. Because of the role played by the Jews as the object of Jesus' own proclamation of himself, it has been cogently argued that John's Gospel was composed as a missionary or evangelistic tract for Jews. There is a great deal to be said both for the general view and for this narrower definition of missionary purpose that confines it to Jews. That there is a strong missionary thrust in the Fourth Gospel is clear enough. Quite possibly earlier forms or constituent parts of the Gospel were written for missionary purposes. For example, the view that the narrative framework and substance of John is based upon an earlier missionary gospel consisting mainly of signs and passion narratives is plausible, if not conclusively demonstrable.[51] That the present form of the Gospel is solely or even primarily evangelical in purpose is, however, questionable.

Two considerations particularly justify reservations on this point. First, and most important, the farewell discourses and Jesus' departing prayer, which in some respects represent the culmination of the Gospel, are addressed to problems and issues that were of concern to Christians per se. While they do not, like the Johannine Epistles, represent the dirty linen of early Christianity which one would dare not air in public, they also do not constitute an appeal for prospective converts.

Second, the conclusion of the Gospel (chap. 20) is ambiguous in this respect. The proof of the resurrection offered Thomas may be considered a missionary argument for the reality of the resurrection, but the final word of Jesus (20:29), which was probably originally intended as his departing word in the Gospel, is a blessing upon Christians (certainly the vast majority of them) who have believed without seeing Jesus. One could construe it as a final word to the reader and prospective convert. On these terms, the Thomas scene then portrays Jesus making a convert at the conclusion of the Gospel. Thomas has challenged him, saying unless certain conditions are fulfilled he will not believe (20:25). These conditions are fulfilled and Thomas confesses Jesus as Lord and God. Yet the figure of Thomas is not entirely appropriate to represent a new convert, since he is already one of the Twelve (20:24). Moreover, he and Philip have raised perplexed questions with Jesus in the farewell discourses (14:4ff.), which seem to find their answer here. Thus, in the context of the Gospel which lies before us, the Thomas scene appears to address itself to intramural Christian questions. It is not impossible, however, that in its original form or as part of an earlier narrative source this scene was primarily intended to have an evangelical, missionary impact upon prospective converts. The statement of purpose in the concluding colophon of 20:30–31, if it was part of an earlier recension or constituent source of the Gospel, may have meant "in order that you may begin to believe . . ." (The aorist subjunctive can properly have ingressive force.) Yet in view of the present character and content of the Gospel too much weight should not be laid upon the aorist verb tense, which in any event does not have to be understood in this way, and may not represent the original reading. There is strong manuscript evidence (B,‭א‬) for the present subjunctive, which could be translated "in order that you may go on believing."

Whatever may be said of the conclusion of chapter 20, the purpose of the account found in chapter 21, which as far as we know has always concluded the published form of the Gospel, is not ambiguous. It not only addresses Christian issues and concerns, but apparently such interests and problems as existed within specific Christian communities. In fact, it is quite possible that chapter 21 was composed to allay certain difficulties which the Fourth Gospel had caused or, it was thought, might cause among Christian readers, that is, *within* the church.

If in general a primary missionary purpose of the Fourth Gospel is subject to doubt, the same dubiety applies to the view that the present Gospel was composed specifically to convert Jews to Christianity.[52] Nevertheless, the emphasis on belief in Jesus' messiahship, the highly concentrated christological focus, and the vigorous rejection of Jesus on the part of the Jews all suggest mission to Jews as an important aspect of the milieu of the Fourth Gospel. Quite possibly some part or parts of it, for example, the sign and passion narratives, were earlier used in an effort to convert Jews. The present form of the Gospel, however, contains significant elements which do not accord well with such a view. Aside from the considerations already mentioned, there are several indications that the Evangelist has in view the universal scope of the Christian gospel. Not the least of these is the climactic scene in 12:20ff. in which the Greeks approach Jesus. Just at this point Jesus announces for the first time in the Gospel that the hour of the glorification of the Son of man has come. Thus it is rather clearly, and historically correctly, implied that the death of Jesus marks the point after which the gospel about him is preached in the Greek, Gentile world. In addition, the sharply polemical tone adopted by Jesus in his controversy with the Jews and their hostile rejection of him do not suggest a missionary, but rather a hostile relationship in which lines have been very sharply drawn. It is as if the Evangelist has already consigned the Jews to the judgment they brought upon themselves in rejecting Jesus. "He came to his own, and his own did not receive him" (1:11). Yet despite the sharpness of the division, there are indications that John still has not given up hope of making conversions among Jews. He speaks almost wistfully of those whose fear of being excluded from the synagogues prevents their confessing their belief in Jesus (9:22; 12:42). Nicodemus, the Pharisee and ruler of the Jews, plays a curiously ambiguous role. His inability to comprehend Jesus evokes the latter's stern rebuke (e.g., 3:10), but the fact that he later appears to defend Jesus to his colleagues on the Sanhedrin (7:50–52) and to participate in his burial (19:39) indicates that his final response to Jesus is at least not negative. Moreover, if "Jew" is often a term of opprobrium, this is not always the case (e.g., 4:22). *Ioudaioi* is generally used in a negative sense, but "Israel" is almost invariably used in a positive one: "A true Israelite in whom there is no guile" (1:47); "a teacher of Israel" (3:10); "the King of Israel" (used of Jesus; 1:49). Even the Pharisees are not entirely disbelieving (9:16). While the Gospel is scarcely rightly viewed as a missionary tract for Jews, the Evangelist and his community have not shut the door to conversions from among the children of Israel.

There seems, however, to be a pronounced leaning in the direction of heterodox Judaism, especially an interest in Samaria and the Samaritans. Not by coincidence is the Samaritan woman, whom Jesus encounters by Jacob's well *in Samaria*, able to understand him better than the learned Nicodemus. If salvation is of the Jews, in the sense that it originates among them, it is received by the Samaritans, while they reject it. The impression gained from the conclusion of the narrative of the woman of Samaria is that the message of the gospel, that Jesus is the "savior of the world," enjoyed considerable success there. This, in fact, accords well with the report of the Samaritan mission in Acts 8. (It is worth observing that apparently Luke is also interested in Samaria and the Samaritan mission; only in Luke 10:30–35 does the parable of the Good Samaritan appear.) There are other evidences of John's interest in Samaria and of affinities with distinctly Samaritan thought.[53] Interestingly, John's positive connections with Judaism are often found to be with heterodox or sectarian forms of the parent religion. In addition to the pro-Samaritan bias there are numerous theological and conceptual parallels with John in literature of the Qumran sect. All of this accords well with the apparent polar opposition between the Fourth Gospel (and Johannine Christianity) and the specifically Pharisaic forms of Jewish life and thought which became dominant in the post-war, post-Jamnian period. It is probably too much to say that Samaritanism per se had a strong and direct influence upon Johannine Christianity. The influence was more subtle and is probably to be explained by the interest among Johannine Christians in promoting a Christian mission in Samaria and among Samaritans. Quite possibly Samaritan converts affected the development of Johannine theology.

Eschatology

In several respects the Gospel of John reflects the influence of the situation and conditions under which Christians lived at the close of the first century. Although the Gospel presents a Christ who seems to stand imperturbable over against the vicissitudes of life, it was nevertheless affected by them. There are problems given by the very fact of the passage of time and the continuation of the ordinary ebb and flow of history.

Contrary to the expectations of many if not most Christians of the first and second generations, Jesus did not return to claim his own, and God did not put an end to the principalities and powers that rule this world, causing the Apostle Paul to speak of "the present evil age" (Gal. 1:4). One has only to read such passages as 1 Thess. 4:13–18 or Mark 13 to understand how lively the expectation of the imminent return of the Lord had been. Probably the passing of the awful, cataclysmic Roman war, in which Jerusalem and the temple were destroyed, without the occurrence of the expected consummation of history, gave many Christians pause. If not then, when? As time elapsed and whole generations passed from the scene, the crisis of the early church became even more acute. The generation of eyewitnesses, who had been with Jesus himself, passed off the scene. The matter of preserving their recollection, tradition, and proclamation of Jesus became a serious one.

In certain ways the early Christians were under the same necessity of retrenchment and consolidation as their Jewish counterparts.[54] The latter had experienced considerable disillusionment in the aftermath of the Roman war. National zeal accompanied by apocalyptic expectation and fervor had been dealt a severe blow. God did not intervene to save his people and put the Romans to flight. Nevertheless, such passions and hopes were once again aroused by the messianic claimant Bar Kochba, only to be shattered once again, this time finally, in the Second Roman War (132–35). Thus, the failure of the Jewish-Roman conflict to bring on the final apocalyptic drama signaling the end or transformation of human history constituted a problem for both Christians and Jews. It was, of course, a less severe difficulty for Christians, who could understand the debacle as God's punishment for the Jews' sin (Luke 21:22). Yet it must have been a matter of no minor consternation to many Jewish Christians that the most holy place in the world should be allowed first to fall under the governance of revolutionary extremists and then literally to fall in ruins before the military might of the pagan Roman Empire.

The continuation of human history without God's direct intervention meant of course that Christians had to come to terms with the prospect of living in the world for a long time, a prospect that doubtless seemed increasingly as inevitable as it may have been disturbing. A number of the later NT writings, especially the Pauline Pastorals and the Johannine letters (which might well be termed the Johannine Pastorals), are very much concerned with the necessity of organizing the church and ordering its life so as to expedite its continued existence and mission in the world. This purpose is to some extent reflected also in the Fourth Gospel, although it is focused less upon problems of a practical, tactical, or even strategic sort than upon the theological problem of the non-occurrence of the parousia of Jesus and its significance and implications for the life and thought of Christians and the church.

While the Fourth Gospel contains references to a "last day" (e.g., 6:39, 40, etc.) that seem to presuppose the return of Jesus, which is in fact explicitly anticipated in 1 John (cf. 2:18, 28; 3:2-3), its emphasis is rather upon the eschatological salvation which has already taken place. In John 3:16-21, esp. 17-18, for example, the reality of the salvation already present in Jesus is underscored. In his presence the eschatological salvation and judgment already impinge effectively upon the world of men. Thus in the Fourth Gospel eternal life is understood not only as life beyond or after physical death, but as a dimension or quality of life that is already a present possibility for the person who believes in Jesus. When Martha, the sister of Lazarus, is assured by Jesus that her brother will live, she answers that she knows that he will rise in the resurrection at the last day (11:24). Jesus then responds with the famous word: "I am the resurrection and the life," as if to correct Martha's misunderstanding of his assurance as referring to a promised resurrection in the indefinite future. The assertion that Jesus is the resurrection and the life is paralleled and elaborated by such statements as are found in 17:3, where Jesus explicitly equates knowledge of himself with eternal life, and 14:6: "I am the way, the truth, and the life."

Although John's eschatology is probably not a direct development either of the synoptic or the Pauline, it can legitimately be understood and explained in relation to them. The Jesus of the synoptic tradition speaks of the kingdom of God as a future reality in most of the instances in which he speaks at all of the time of the kingdom's appearing or coming. There are, of course, many instances in which Jesus speaks of the kingdom without specifying its futurity, and occasionally he speaks as if this kingdom might already be present. But if we consider only the synoptic references to the kingdom, not the Pauline and the Johannine, we are left with the impression that the kingdom is not yet here, but will arrive soon. This is especially the case if the kingdom is viewed in relation to the many sayings of Jesus about the coming, apocalyptic Son of man.

Something of the same perspective is also conveyed by Paul. He does not characteristically speak of the coming of the kingdom, however, but of the return of Jesus and the gathering together of his followers (1 Thess. 4:13–18; 1 Cor. 15:20–28). Eschatological salvation (and salvation remains by definition eschatological) is by and large still future for Paul. Yet a significant shift has taken place. Paul understands the eschatological pronouncement of judgment, that is, the judgment of acquittal which God pronounces over those who have faith in Jesus, to be rendered in the present age. Thus those who have been justified, that is, pronounced righteous, in the act of faith have peace with God (Rom. 5:1). This peace is not simple absence of tension or hostility; it is the eschatological state of reconciliation which bestows freedom from the bondage of sin and death. Yet for Paul the eschatological realities are present in no other sense than this. Salvation as the power and presence of God's rule and the realization of possibilities for life inherent in God is principally still to come, still future. Paul understands this future in the conceptual terms of post-biblical, Jewish apocalyptic.

Precisely on this point the Fourth Gospel marks what might well be considered an advance in eschatology beyond Paul. For John salvation is already present as eternal life. This understanding of it is not entirely an innovation, since the life of the kingdom of God can be described as "eternal life" even in the synoptic tradition. Yet the unequivocal affirmation that this life is a present, as well as a future, possibility and that it is nothing other than knowledge of Jesus Christ is indeed a Johannine innovation. Whereas Paul is reticent to describe the new life in Christ as the *fulfillment* of eschatological possibilities in the present age, John seems eager to do just this. Moreover, he views as inadequate a Christian doctrine of salvation and eschatology that remains within the temporal and conceptual framework of Jewish—and early Christian—apocalyptic. John does not deny Christians the consolation of hope for eternal life after death, but he insists on, and lays heavy emphasis upon, the present possibility of that life. In fact, he would apparently be willing to say that whoever does not have that eschatological life in his earthly existence will not have it ever.

Remnants of the older apocalyptic eschatology abound in John's Gospel. For example, the farewell discourses recall the apocalyptic discourses of the synoptic Gospels in their content as well as their position in the Gospel. Jesus speaks to his disciples of the things that are to come, including his own future coming to them and presence with them. But John tends to refer this whole future dimension to the time of the church rather than to the apocalyptic endtime. In other words, Jesus speaks not of the manifestation of the Son of man at the end of the age, but of the manifestation of the Son of God, immediately upon his resurrection and thereafter, to the church of his disciples. Thus Judas asks, "How is it that you will manifest yourself to us and not to the world?" (14:22). In answering, Jesus accepts the premise of the question and describes the mystical and non-physical, non-apocalyptic, manner of his presence (14:23–24) among his disciples. While the Fourth Gospel does not deny the ancient Christian belief in the return of Jesus at the end of the age and at points seems to assume it, it scarcely gives that belief clear and unambiguous support. Thus at the conclusion of the farewell discourses, and particularly in the final prayer, Jesus does not promise to return in triumph over the world. Rather he says, "I have overcome the world" (16:33), and in his concluding petition for the disciples prays that they may finally be with him and behold his primordial glory (17:24). Jesus does not come again to where his disciples have been; rather he comes and takes them to where he is. His coming is best understood as a personal and spiritual advent, not an apocalyptic drama.

But this coming again of Jesus is not reserved for the death of each individual disciple, as if he should have his own private and personal parousia. Instead, Jesus promises his continuing presence with his church. John moves boldly in reformulating Christian eschatology and in effect addresses two theological problems. Not only does his new interpretation of Jesus' coming again resolve anxiety over the failure of the expected apocalyptic eschatological conditions to appear, it also affords a perspective for dealing with the question of his relation to his disciples in view of the prospect of his indefinite physical absence from them. Jesus does return and abide with his disciples, claims the Evangelist, worldly appearances to the contrary notwithstanding.

Jesus and the Spirit

It is obviously not satisfactory to the Evangelist, nor to the Christian circles from which he comes, simply to say that Jesus remains with his disciples in the tradition of his words and deeds, although there was such a tradition available to him, particularly a narrative tradition. Rather the Evangelist seeks to assure his readers of the continuing, living presence of Jesus. As we have seen, references in the farewell discourses to Jesus' return have about them a certain ambiguity. The language evokes the older Christian tradition and expectation of the apocalyptic return of Jesus, but on closer scrutiny the text actually seems to refer to Jesus' return and presence after the crucifixion, that is, in the resurrection (e.g., 16:16–28). Yet an ambiguity remains, for in the farewell discourses Jesus always speaks of the resurrection indirectly. In fact, the Fourth Gospel contains no such explicit predictions of the resurrection as resurrection such as are found in the synoptic passion predictions. (10:17–18 is a veiled allusion to the resurrection, but the specific resurrection language is avoided.) From much of what is said in the Gospel one receives the impression that Jesus returns directly to his divine glory through the crucifixion. Yet the resurrection is so firmly a part of the Jesus tradition, including John's community's tradition, that he does not think to ignore it. And, in fact, the theological truth which it represents is of indispensable importance to him. Jesus' death is not the end of his ministry, but rather the beginning of a broader and more effective one, and the resurrection marks its beginning point.

Yet there is here again a curious ambiguity in the Fourth Gospel. Appar-

ently the Evangelist does not want to say that the risen Jesus remained with
his disciples indefinitely or for a very long period. Later Gnostic texts give
place for revelations of Jesus by allowing him to remain with his disciples for
years after his initial resurrection appearances. Herein lay a framework and
an enormous potential for heretical developments, inasmuch as the risen Jesus
could communicate to his disciples as revelation the full range of Gnostic
teaching. John does not go in this direction. In his account Jesus' tomb is first
found empty as in the synoptics. Then Jesus appears to Mary Magdalene outside the tomb (John 20:11–18), as in Matthew he appears to the women who
have discovered the tomb empty (Matt. 28:8–10). Uniquely Johannine, however, is Jesus' forbidding Mary to touch him because he has not yet ascended
and his command to tell his brethren (cf. Matt. 28:10) that he is ascending to
God. Probably Jesus' subsequent invitation to Thomas to touch him (20:25)
indicates that the ascension has already taken place. Thus in John 20:22 (as
in Acts 2) it is the ascended Jesus who bestows the Spirit. Yet there is a difference between the appearances to the Twelve and the continuing presence of
Jesus among his disciples. Jesus' final word to Thomas, the benediction pronounced upon those who do not see and yet believe, clearly implies that the
normal experience of the believer and the post-resurrection church does not
include *visions* of the risen Lord. Otherwise, there would be no problem occa-
sioned by the absence of Jesus from his disciples and the non-occurrence of
the parousia or second coming; but that such a problem does exist seems
clearly attested by the farewell discourses. Moreover, a Christianity based
upon such psychic or other phenomena would soon lose touch with the historical reality of Jesus, and that the Evangelist clearly does not want to do, despite
the apparent liberties he takes with the tradition. Not the risen Jesus, but the
Spirit which he sends, assures his continuing presence among his disciples.

The presupposition of John's way of dealing with this problem or set of
problems is the experienced reality of the Holy Spirit among Christians, in
the church. That the gift and gifts of the Spirit were generally acknowledged
phenomena in the early church scarcely needs to be demonstrated. Already
Paul, who himself experiences the Spirit and, indeed, speaks in tongues, seeks
to align his understanding of the Spirit with the will of God in Christ without
necessarily quenching its more exuberant manifestations or suppressing those
who manifest them. Already for Paul the Spirit is the source of encouragement, consolation, and life in Christ, but the experience per se, if not subject
to the word and discipline of the gospel, represents a potential menace to its
truth and to decency and order in the church. A not dissimilar situation existed
in the Johannine churches. Thus the author of 1 John warns against believing
every spirit and underlines the necessity of testing the spirits (4:1ff.), at the
same time acknowledging that the Spirit is the means or mode by which
believers are assured of the presence of Jesus Christ among them (3:24; 4:13).
In a situation where heresy threatens, Spirit possession and Spirit-inspired

utterances represent a potential danger, but they do not call into question the necessity and importance of the work of the Spirit, properly perceived and understood. Probably the Revelation to John presents a literary deposit of such Spirit-inspired prophecy as is referred to elsewhere in early Christian writings. While one can scarcely any longer claim that Revelation is the work of the same author(s) as the Gospel and letters, some striking affinities with the Gospel have long been noted (p. 14 above).

By means of the Paraclete sayings the farewell discourses point forward, albeit anachronistically, to the post-resurrection era, in which Jesus will come and expatiate upon the historical revelation already given. They do not, however, promise new revelations in distinction from what has already been said, except perhaps in 16:12–13. But even there the concern to tie what the Paraclete will say to Jesus is obvious (v. 13). We may, in fact, see just a bit of unresolved ambiguity in the Gospel at this point. Clearly the Paraclete, the Spirit, continues to mediate the truth of Jesus to the church of his disciples, and in such a way that they are not alone. They are not without the guidance, comfort and sustenance (bread and water of life!) that he gives. What the Paraclete says he says on the authority of Jesus and his historical revelation. Yet the Paraclete is not just the guardian of the Jesus tradition. His function is not to pass that tradition along without emendation and alteration. It is a fair inference from the character and content of the speech of Jesus in the Gospel that the Spirit authorizes new words of Jesus for new and unprecedented times. That the Gospel of John represents the general tenor and bearing of such Spirit-inspired utterances of Christ, delivered through prophets (such as John of Patmos!) seems likely, especially in view of the character of the words of Jesus found in the Gospel (so different are they from any other early Jesus tradition) and the statements about the function of the Paraclete, as well as the evidence of 1 John and Revelation.

The relationship of the Johannine letters to the Gospel of John is a matter about which there is still disagreement and debate. We have adopted the position that the letters are secondary in time and interests to the Gospel. Certainly they represent more explicitly the situation and problems of a developing institution. The relationship of the Apocalypse to the other Johannine writings is, and probably will remain, a matter that defies close definition, although its reality is as hard to deny as it is to specify. By way of hypothesis, however, an ordering of these documents with respect to Spirit inspiration in a rough sort of history of the Johannine tradition or school may prove useful and suggestive.

When this is done the Apocalypse seems obviously the earliest, with respect to traditional content if not actual time of composition. The words of the heavenly Christ are given as such; the role and identity of the prophet are specified; the apocalyptic tenor of the book as a whole, as well as specific scenes, bespeaks its primitive character. No effort is made to adduce any criteria to support the claim that these are really words of the heavenly Christ. The author appeals only to his inspiration, which cannot be tested, and denounces and threatens anyone who should add to or subtract from his inspired book.

The Gospel, on the other hand, manifests a marked absence of apocalyptic perspective and coloration, although it seems to address a constituency in which such interests have been alive, and, perhaps, disappointed. It was certainly published for such a constituency (cf. 21:22–23). Spirit-inspired words of the heavenly Jesus are now placed on the lips of the historical figure from the past, a procedure which fits the absence of an apocalyptic, future-oriented frame of reference. They have to do no longer with the outpouring of wrath at the imminent end or with warnings pertaining thereto. Instead they are directed to disciples, a church, which must continue to live in the physical absence of Jesus in a hostile world. In the Paraclete sayings Jesus is made to promise just the kind of extension of his revelatory work that is, in all probability, represented in the discourses of the Gospel. Yet the continuity of this work with the historical revelation which the Gospel purports to describe is strongly affirmed. Nevertheless, the boundaries or criteria by which the continuing revelatory work is to be limited or judged are not clearly specified. Presumably they are to be derived from the traditions and conceptualization of Jesus alive in the community. The potentially problematic character of this disposition of the matter may then come to light in the Johannine letters, which in this matter particularly seem to be subsequent to the Gospel.

First John inveighs against what is apparently a docetic christological heresy and appeals to authoritative belief and tradition. We have observed the writer's warning that not every spirit is to be believed, but that spirits—that is, as is specifically indicated, false prophets (4:1) claiming to speak in the Spirit—are to be tested. But he is apparently unable to bring to bear a sizable body of tradition as criteria for testing the spirits. His principal traditional norms are the orthodox confession that Jesus Christ has come in the flesh (4:2–3; cf. 2:22), which is anti-docetic in thrust, and the now old commandment (2:6–11) of brotherly love, which Jesus gave his disciples in the Fourth Gospel (13:34; 15:12; cf. 1 John 3:23; 4:21). In any event, it is doubtless not coincidental that we find in rapid and uninterrupted sequence in 1 John: the love commandment cited as a command of Christ (3:23); reference to the reassuring role of the Spirit (3:24); the injunction to test the spirits to see if they are from God because of the many false prophets abroad (4:1); and the anti-docetic confession as the test of whether or not a spirit is in fact from God (4:2–3).

Whether this ordering of the Johannine writings corresponds to the actual historical sequence, we may never know. It is nevertheless a plausible one, in that the evidence of spirit-inspiration and the accompanying problem of criteria or norms fits rather well a chronological sequence which on other grounds appears likely.

To sum up, the Gospel of John arose out of a tradition and community which understood itself to be rooted in the ministry of Jesus himself and authorized by some apostolic or equivalent authority. This Johannine Christianity was a relatively independent development of the NT period, but not without significant contact or similarity with synoptic and Pauline traditions and versions of the gospel. That the Johannine community was driven by a strong missionary effort, first and perhaps for several decades directed to Jews, is a reasonable inference from the Gospel's emphasis upon the importance of attaining faith in Jesus. Yet in its present form the Fourth Gospel is not primarily a missionary gospel. In its final recension a heavy emphasis on Christian theological and related matters is evident, as well as a sharp disjuncture and hostile stance toward Judaism. In this and other respects the Gospel reflects the setting and problems of Christianity at the end of the first century. Among the more pressing theological problems, none was greater than the delay in Jesus' expected return and the consequent necessity of facing and understanding theologically an indefinite period in which the disciples, the church, would have to co-exist with and in the world. John presents a solution to this problem by presenting Jesus without the apocalyptic conceptuality of the synoptic tradition. His message in John has to do with christological issues and the present possibility of eternal life rather than with the imminent kingdom of God. The physical absence of Jesus from the church, which must remain in the world, is not denied. Nevertheless, the resurrection is presented as the point at which Jesus' presence and ministry through the Spirit begins. The Spirit-Paraclete becomes the means through which the revelation of Christ is unfolded and mediated. This theological position presupposes a vital faith in, and experience of, the reality of the Spirit, already attested elsewhere in the Revelation of John. Such reliance upon the Spirit becomes problematic to the degree that criteria for discerning what claims for, or of, the Spirit are valid expressions of the revelation of Jesus Christ are lacking. The problem is recognized and an attempt is made to deal with it in 1 John.

CHAPTER NINE

UNDERSTANDING THE GOSPEL OF JOHN
AS LITERATURE

Up to this point we have looked at the Johannine literature, and the Fourth Gospel particularly, from the standpoint of the historical-critical method. This does not mean that we have been concerned only with historical questions and not with matters of interpretation. Indeed, our treatment exemplifies the fact that historical-critical exegesis has increasingly focused on the interpretation of the biblical writings as documents of their own times, places, and circumstances. As we have seen, historical reconstruction of those circumstances is itself a matter of the interpretation of the data provided by those documents together with other relevant information from late antiquity and the early Christian world. Without abandoning that method or perspective, we now turn away from it deliberately, in order to look at the Gospel of John from a somewhat different, if not unrelated, point of view.

A most promising new approach to the Gospel of John takes up the original maxim of biblical criticism, namely, that the Bible should be read like any other literature, and asks how other literatures are now being read. Of particular interest and importance is recent work in the analysis and criticism of narrative. Such work has been derived from, and applied to, modern narrative, particularly fiction, but it is not without relevance to the Gospels, which are also narratives. In certain respects redaction criticism has paved the way for the application of such perspectives and insights by its insistence that the evangelists were all authors, each in his own way. The earlier view that the Gospels were *Kleinliteratur, Volksbücher* (popular writings) rather than works of literature properly speaking had carried with it the corollary that they were not accessible to a higher literary criticism. It is, however, no longer obvious that the Gospels are not literature or the evangelists not authors.[55] However that may be, the Gospels are, in fact, narratives, the question of their historicity and the literary aspirations of the authors aside. It is worth asking how modern insights into the nature of narrative as well as ancient criteria for understanding narrative match up with and illumine them.

In a recent monograph, *Anatomy of the Fourth Gospel*, R. Alan Culpepper has carefully and helpfully shown how insights from such work on the nature of narrative may be applied to the Gospel of John. In his foreword to *Anatomy* Frank Kermode, the noted English critic, whose work on the Gospel of Mark has had a wide impact, writes: "This book strongly upholds the position, long since enunciated but still widely ignored or disputed, that there can be no sharp distinction between sacred and profane hermeneutics."[56] Thus Culpepper belongs in the great, and original, tradition of biblical criticism.

Narratological analysis of the Fourth Gospel will not be a totally new world to anyone familiar with literary criticism, even as it has been traditionally applied to the Bible. As far as the Fourth Gospel is concerned, it does not generate insights radically opposed to those represented thus far in this book. Talk of plot, characters, irony, misunderstanding, and symbolism sounds familiar enough. What is new and different is a commitment to understanding the narrative world of the Fourth Gospel on its own terms. The text is viewed not as a "window," whether on the events narrated or the setting from which the Gospel emerged, but as a "mirror." That is, meaning is not derived from looking through the text to historical or other realities, but from the interaction of text and reader.[57]

Because such a concept of the meaning of texts has been worked out mainly in relation to narrative of fiction, it is at least arguable that the biblical writings differ decisively. Historically or theologically they are to point beyond themselves. Such considerations may ultimately have a bearing on the undertaking, but they do not negate it from the outset. How a narrative text works, how it is read and appropriated, is not necessarily related to whether it is fictional or historical. In fact, it could be argued that the Fourth Gospel is in many of its specifics fictional and yet by intention profoundly historical. But apart from such an observation, the critical analysis of how a narrative text works is not necessarily tied to the question of whether it is fictional or historical. That question is, of course, important for understanding its origin, and biblical criticism has long been preoccupied with questions of origin. Texts such as the Gospel of John can, however, be read without such preoccupations and without prejudice to the matter of their historicity.

Author, Implied Author, and Narrator

When this is done, it is most illuminating and instructive to see the effect upon the traditional historical-critical treatment of authorship and audience or intended readers. The dictum that the better we understand the author, his situation and purpose, and the better we understand the intended readers, their situation, and questions, the better we can understand a document has long been the fundamental assumption of biblical exegesis. As long as we are considering a communication such as a letter, for example 1 Corinthians, and want to know what the letter writer intended to say, that assumption is unassailable. With a Gospel, however, we have a literary product which stands on its own, in which the situations of the author and his readers are not so obvious; they do not obtrude in the same way. The author may or may not have intended to address a specific set of readers and their distinct situation, needs, or questions.

In this connection one might observe that a great deal of modern gospel exegesis has actually proceeded on the basis of assumptions derived from the exegesis of Paul's epistles. It is sometimes assumed that the Gospels are theological documents addressed to specific situations in the early church. To interpret them is to understand what those situations were and how the evangelists sought to address them. Without negating the important insight and truth contained in this approach, one can sense its difficulty by simply observing the variety of theories of origin and purpose that have in recent decades been propounded about each Gospel. It will be worthwhile at least provisionally to put aside preoccupations with historical origin and purpose in order to appreciate critically the Fourth Gospel as a mirror text. One may, of course, always return to the question of whether, or in what sense, the Fourth Gospel may also be a window, either to the events it purports to narrate or to the circumstances and setting of its origins. In any event, the Gospels are narratives and may be analyzed by the means and methods appropriate to that general genre.

When one asks about the author of the Fourth Gospel, he may open up the question of the Gospel's apparent identification of the author with the Beloved Disciple and the church's ancient tradition, according to which that illustrious figure was John the Son of Zebedee. Unlike the synoptic Gospels, John has something directly to say about its authorship (21:24), although what is said has seemingly been the occasion of more disagreement and confusion than clarity. The identity of the author remains unknown. Because of this, most recent exegesis has simply bracketed out the question of authorship as insoluble and in any case unessential for the interpretation of the document. At the same time inferences about what the purpose of the Evangelist may have been continue to be made in the circular process of determining what the Evangelist meant to say to his intended readers.

In the analysis of any narrative, such as John's Gospel, one is aware of an author. But the author does not stand within the text, even though it may contain references or allusions to him. The actual author and the actual reader stand at opposite poles, so to speak, outside the text. Within the narrative text there is a narrator, who tells the story, and the narratee to whom it is told. They may be named or remain anonymous. In the case of the Gospels they remain anonymous. On the other hand, in Thornton Wilder's play *Our Town*, for example, the narrator, who tells the story, is very much in evidence, although the narratee is not. In the film *Amadeus* Salieri is the narrator and a priest is nominally the narratee. (The original play, however, had no such narratee, Salieri speaking directly to the audience.) To cite a biblical example, in Acts 26 the narrator of the story of Paul's conversion is Paul, the narratee is Herod Agrippa. In that case the reader is allowed to overhear what Paul tells.

In the Gospel of John no narrator is introduced as such, nor is a narratee. Yet there is a voice that tells the story, that narrates, and that there will be listeners-readers is assumed. Thus on occasion the narrator will tell the reader something he needs to know in order to appreciate better what is going on (e.g., 2:22; 7:39; 12:33). Throughout the Gospel the narrator reveals aspects of his own perspective and point of view. His is anything but a value-free, unbiased account of Jesus' ministry. To cite but the simplest example, the Gospel's prologue reveals immediately a high estimate of the meaning and significance of Jesus. In revealing so much the narrator delivers by implication the perspective of an author. Thus one may speak not only of an author standing outside the text and a narrator who delivers the text, but also of an implied author, who is implied in, or maybe inferred from, the text. Redaction-critical and other related interpretations of the Fourth Gospel have, as we know, inferred a great deal already about the real author, his setting and purpose, and the circumstances he addressed. The inferences drawn from the Gospel give such efforts the ring of plausibility, if not the stamp of certainty. The analysis of narrative stops short, however, of claiming for these inferences historical validity or status. What may certainly be inferred from the many hints and suggestions of the narrative is an implied author. By the same token, similar evocation of the situation of the Gospels' apparent intended readers suggests the clear silhouette of an implied reader, as well as the circumstances under which the author addressed that reader. The voice of the narrator implies an author, and what is said to or about the narratee a reader. The implied author or implied reader may or may not correspond with the real author and the real first-century (or twentieth-century) reader, but the chances are that there is correspondence in both cases. Otherwise, the Gospel is in some sense misleading, if not a hoax. That is, the many cues and clues it gives for its interpretation would not correspond to a setting in any real world.

To give a concrete illustration, the characterization of Jesus' opponents as "the Jews" reflects, as we have noticed, a historical period some decades after Jesus' ministry. By the same token, the statements about those who confess Christ being put out of the synagogue imply a similar period and apparently a situation in which followers of Jesus were being expelled from synagogues for their allegiance to him, or feared they would be. Conceivably, the narrative refers to no historical reality, whether in Jesus' time, the author's, or in between. Conceivably, there was no threat, real or perceived, of being put out of the synagogue for confessing Jesus, in which case the Gospel's portrayal of the Jews and obvious bias against them would be unmotivated and gratuitous. If that were the case the contemporary critical reader would be deceived not only about Jesus, but also about the circumstances of the author and the implied reader. In a real sense both the implied author and the implied reader would be misleading constructs of the real author.

That they may be such misleading constructs is possible, but unlikely. The strong polemical tenor of so much of the Fourth Gospel warrants the belief that it is derived from the historically real and concrete circumstances that the narrative suggests. Moreover, that the conflict with the Jews, who are frequently called Pharisees and who seem to be in charge of synagogues, is cast in terms of a conflict directly with Jesus suggests that the author believed that there was a conflict and that it was fundamentally the same conflict in which Jesus was involved. The question has always been christological, or so the Gospel insists. That is, it has from the beginning been a matter of what one makes of Jesus and how one relates to him. All this could be a fiction, but common sense and a reasonable view of any real author's purpose and integrity implies that it is not. But however that may be, the literary analysis of the Gospel narrative can establish the position of the implied author and the implied reader while leaving open the question of whether or how they relate to the origin, historical setting, and purpose of the Gospel.

Narrative World, Plot, and Characters

Analysis of the narrative world of the Gospel reveals other interesting aspects and features of the narrative that conventional criticism and exegesis have overlooked. Culpepper has made some intriguing calculations about the time period covered by the narrative, the nature of the plot, the role of the characters, and the way the Gospel leads and directs the reader through "implicit commentary."

It is commonly and rightly noted that in the Gospel of John Jesus' ministry extends over three Passovers (2:14; 6:4; 13:1) and thus a period of between two and three years. Almost no one, however, has paid attention to how much of this period is actually covered in the narrative. For example, the year between the Passover week of 2:14—3:21 and the mention of the next Passover in 6:4 is represented by the narration of events that would scarcely encompass more than a couple of weeks. Culpepper calculates that the scenes narrated from the second year cover about a month. On the other hand, John 12—20 deals with a period of only two weeks, and chapters 13—19 with a single twenty-four-hour day. As the narrative approaches and reaches the final climactic events of Jesus' career it "slows down" drastically.[58] This is, of course, true of all the Gospels. It is another way of stating what Martin Kähler long ago observed when he characterized the Gospels as passion narratives with extended introductions.

Other temporal aspects of the narrative of the Fourth Gospel are worth observing. To an extent unparalleled in the other Gospels, John refers backward in the narrative to things already said and done ("analepses") and forward to events still to transpire ("prolepses").[59] The analepses may refer to things which have occurred within the time-frame of the narrative ("internal analepses") or to events lying outside, that is, prior to, the beginning of the narrative ("external analepses"). For example, John the Baptist's references to his initial meeting with Jesus (1:19–34) are in the form of external analepses. He is announcing events that have already occurred, outside and prior to the narrative proper, as distinguished from the prologue. On the other hand, Jesus' reference to his previous miracle (7:21–23) narrated in chapter 5 (thus "internal" to the time of the narrative) is also a "repeating analepsis," since it refers to something already narrated in the Gospel. What is said of analepses may be applied *mutatis mutandis* to prolepses. The Evangelist's statement in 7:39 that the Spirit had not yet been given because Jesus was not yet glorified qualifies as a "mixed" prolepsis. That is, it is completed partly within the narrative (internal prolepses) in that the disciples receive the Holy Spirit in 20:22. Yet disciples at the time the Gospel was written (including the readers), in the time between, and presumably on into the future may receive the Spirit (external prolepses). Thus its fulfillment lies beyond the narrative time of the Gospel as well as within it.

Anyone who has studied English literature has dealt with plot and characters. Biblical exegetes, however, have not usually thought in those terms, at least not in a systematic way. Probably they have not because of the historicist legacy of biblical research, which for years made questions of historical actuality or accuracy primary and, with some reason, regarded plot as representing the course of actual events and the "characters" as historical personages. As redaction criticism has moved in the direction of understanding the Gospels on their own terms, however, issues of plot and character, or characterization, have begun to emerge. Interest has focused increasingly on what the evangelists intended to accomplish in the ways in which they shaped the narrative and dealt with the characters.

Just the matter of the source and nature of the so-called Gospel genre, which NT exegetes have focused upon recently, is significantly related to the narrative plots of the Gospels. Genre and plot are obviously not the same. But if there is fundamentally one gospel plot, all the Gospels apparently share the same genre. But do they have the same plot? Obviously, they both do and do not. The death of Jesus is the climactic moment in all the Gospels, the event that imparts movement and direction to the narrative. Yet the way in which it does that differs significantly between Mark and John, for example. In Mark the death of Jesus is rooted in the opposition of evil men who plot against him (3:6) because he performs miracles on the Sabbath. Similarly, Sabbath-breaking is also the cause of deadly hostility in John (5:16–18). In John, however, Jesus' Sabbath-breaking is tied to his claims of a unique filial relationship to God in ways different from the synoptics. As the narrative progresses Mark has Jesus predict his suffering and death as Son of man (8:33; 9:31; 10:33–34), but no very clear motivation for the arrest of Jesus, other than that the

Son of man must suffer (cf. 14:21), and suffer for the benefit of many (14:22–25), is given. The chief priests and scribes plot his arrest and death (14:1), but we are not told why. Only in the trial scene (14:55–62) are charges pertaining to Jesus' threatening the temple brought, and even then they are not sustained. Jesus is rather condemned on the spot for affirming his messianic role and reign (14:61–64).

In John the question of Jesus' messianic claims—not only their assertion but their character—dominates the narrative, as they are repeatedly opposed and rejected by those who are called Jews. There is, however, no trial before the Sanhedrin comparable to Mark 14:55–62. Yet the reasons for Jesus' arrest in John are made quite clear before the event (11:45–53). His raising of Lazarus from the dead (chapter 11), which is not mentioned in Mark or in any of the synoptic Gospels, is an event of public notoriety. Caiaphas warns that if Jesus is allowed to continue to work such signs the Romans will intervene to the detriment of the temple and the nation. Accordingly, Caiaphas advises that it is expedient that one man, Jesus, should die for the people and the whole nation not perish. The stage is thus carefully laid for Jesus' arrest, trial, and execution. John's plot shows a refinement and a development beyond Mark's. Yet the reader does not need to know Mark in order to appreciate John. If the reader does know Mark (Matthew or Luke), however, John seems to address questions that Mark leaves unresolved or to fill lacunae in the narration of the plot.

To pun only slightly, because John gives a fuller narration of the opposition's plotting, he has a more satisfactory and satisfying plot. Perhaps, it is the same plot, but John's narrative gives it a quite distinctive and unique character. We earlier noted how modern scholarship has puzzled over the question of whether the Fourth Evangelist knew, and presupposed, Mark or the other synoptics. Certainly he knew traditions, perhaps a traditional or earlier narration of the ministry of Jesus. Narratological analysis shows by reason of what John presupposes as well as the "gaps" in his narrative that this is the case. But that John knew or presupposed one or more of our other Gospels remains, at least on this basis, uncertain. Nevertheless, it is fair to say that John is of the same genre and possesses a similar plot.

Characterization in the Fourth Gospel goes beyond the synoptics. One might point to the role the various minor characters, many of whom are apparently unknown to the other evangelists, play in the narrative: Nicodemus, the Woman of Samaria, Philip, Thomas, the Man Born Blind. Then there are the significant roles played by Peter and the Beloved Disciple, who frequently appear concurrently, if not in rivalry with one another. Peter is, of course, prominent in all the canonical Gospels, but the Beloved Disciple is not mentioned elsewhere. (In part to remedy this unbearable oversight he has traditionally been identified with John the Son of Zebedee.) In John the Beloved Disciple is the model for all believers in his relationship to Jesus. The disciples as a group stand over against the Jews as a group. While it is possible to say that the characterization of the one is positive and the other negative, that is too simple a description to do justice to the shadings and nuances of the Fourth Gospel. The disciples believe, by definition (2:11), but within the narrative they fall away and desert Jesus. The Jews as a whole do not believe, but Nicodemus represents the recurring possibility that individual Jews, even "rulers" of the Jews (12:42), will believe, and confess their loyalty to him.

The distinctiveness of characterization in the Fourth Gospel can best be seen in the portrayal of Jesus. "In John, the character of Jesus is static; it does not change. He only emerges more clearly as what he is from the beginning."[60] While others change, Jesus remains constant. This fact alone speaks worlds about Johannine Christology. John's characterization of Jesus differs from the other Gospels, although perhaps not so much as was once thought. So-called liberal lives of Jesus attempted to trace a growth or development in Jesus' self-consciousness through the character portrayed in the synoptic Gospels (assuming, of course, the fundamental historicity of that characterization). In, or behind, that character such a development was thought to be discernible. In fact, there is little ground for seeing in any of the Gospels a significant change in the figure or character of Jesus during the course of his ministry.[61] At the same time, the much more human portrait of Jesus that we find in the synoptics suggests that possibility. To modern sensibilities, at least, it does not seem farfetched. The Fourth Gospel, on the other hand, would obviously never permit the most fleeting suggestion of any change in Jesus. In the beginning was the Word, and the Word became flesh. Subsequently, Jesus' relationship of complete and constant dependence upon, and unity with, the Father clearly marks him off from other people. Christians have traditionally read each Gospel in light of the others, particularly the synoptics in light of the Johannine portrait with its explicit and implicit Christology. But Jesus as literary character in John differs markedly from the figure we find in the other Gospels.

Other characters have significance only insofar as they stand in relation to Jesus. This is clearly true of the disciples and of the Jews. The various characters serve either to highlight the character and significance of Jesus or to represent various possible responses to him with which the reader can identify or from which he can learn. Nicodemus (chap. 3) is obviously a Jew, a leader and a representative of the Pharisaic persuasion, who is initially receptive to Jesus. But his judgments about Jesus are based on well-established traditional criteria, which permit him to perceive Jesus' divine origin and mission, but blind him to his radical or revolutionary significance. The Samaritan woman, disreputable on religious and moral grounds, nevertheless fares better. Precisely because she does not know as much she can know more about Jesus. The disciples as individuals and as a group leave something to be desired, and this is true of Peter as well as Philip, Thomas, and the rest. The outstanding exception is, of course, the anonymous Beloved Disciple, whose responses to Jesus are always appropriate. But Lazarus is also beloved of Jesus; Nathanael is a true Israelite; and an unnamed Jerusalemite whose sight has been restored insists on the reality of what Jesus has done for him. Significantly, members of the Twelve known from the synoptics come off less well than other disciples in John.

Misunderstanding, Irony, and Symbolism

What is called the "implicit commentary" of the Gospel, namely, the motif of misunderstanding, the ever-recurring irony, and the symbolism, has perhaps received more attention from conventional exegesis than characteristic aspects of the narrative per se, which have been more or less taken for granted. In all probability this is because these aspects of the Gospels have been singled out for special attention by exegetes who were bent on expounding the message or theology of the Fourth Gospel.

The misunderstandings are, as we have already observed, typical of the Fourth Gospel. Jesus makes a statement capable of being understood in more than one way. His interlocutor(s) responds so as to reveal that he does not understand Jesus' true meaning (cf. 2:20–22). If Jesus says "Destroy this temple, and in three days I will raise it up," his opponents presume he is talking about the edifice in which they are standing and quite naturally express astonishment and disbelief. The narrator then intervenes to say that Jesus was speaking of the temple of his body. Typically, he goes on to suggest that even the disciples did not attain a proper understanding of what had transpired until after Jesus' resurrection. What is the key to the misunderstanding? It has been suggested that Jesus speaks of heavenly realities, while his hearers misunderstand in terms of this world. Culpepper rightly rejects this characterization as too narrow, pointing out that the theme that appears most frequently in the misunderstandings is Jesus' death, resurrection, and glorification, as in the case of the example just cited. "The meaning of this event lies at the heart of the narrator's ideological point of view, and his interpretation of it reflects his temporal position."[62] The interlocutors, including the disciples, stand on the other side of, that is, before, Jesus' death and exaltation. The Evangelist, Jesus, and by implication the reader, stand on this side, and are thus in a position to interpret or understand the true meaning of what is said. The misunderstandings as they are cleared up by the narrator or by Jesus himself tend to draw the reader into the circle of "insiders," those who understand what is going on. They assist the reader in understanding how the Gospel is to be read. One either follows this lead or is put off by the Gospel. As members of a Christian community the readers would possess the basis for understanding. The misunderstandings elicit a nod of affirmation from readers and confirm them in what they already know.

The misunderstandings further reflect the irony of the Fourth Gospel. They exemplify the multiple levels of meaning that are the hallmark of irony. Typically, the narrator, Jesus, and the reader see the true level of meaning, while to Jesus' interlocutors it is invisible or obscure. The interlocutors do not sense the contrast between appearance and reality upon which the irony of the Gospel turns. They do not see that Jesus is talking about birth from above (chap. 3), not simply natural rebirth; about a living water that does not have physical properties, not running water (chap. 4); about a bread that is Jesus himself, not a material bread, not even manna from heaven (chap. 6). They take the outward form to be the reality, when it is not, and boldly voice their profound misunderstandings. The reader appreciates the altogether predictable reactions and enjoys their comic aspect as he is confirmed in the truth that is conveyed. Johannine irony appears, of course, in other ways. Speakers confidently announce truths of which they have no inkling, because they do not really understand what they are saying. At the turning point of the narrative, Caiaphas proclaims the necessity of Jesus' death for the people (11:50) in the most spectacular instance of this phenomenon, but there are others (e.g., 7:35; 8:22).

Major symbols of the Gospel such as bread and water are implicated in the Johannine misunderstandings and irony. Jesus is the true food and drink, in contrast with what people in their ignorance seek. If Jesus is the Light of the World (8:12), his illumination contrasts with the darkness that lies all around (1:5), out of which Nicodemus emerges (3:2) and into which Judas Iscariot withdraws (13:30). The light does not figure quite so directly in Johannine misunderstanding and irony. Yet at the conclusion of the episode of the restoration of sight to the man born blind Jesus says that he has come that those who do not see may see and that those who see may become blind (9:39), whereupon the Pharisees ask him whether they are blind. The conversation manifests multiple levels of meaning. Obviously Jesus is not going about physically blinding people. The imagery of sight and blindness is closely akin to that of light and darkness. It is not necessary to dwell on John's symbolism, because it has long been obvious to exegetes, indeed, to any perceptive reader of the Gospel. Through it the narrative suggests the ways in which Jesus is the reality of authentic life, who transforms and sustains all who come into contact with and receive him.

John offers a persuasive, consistent, and powerful narrative, which is conceived in such a way as to elicit a strong response. The reader will likely be carried along by the Gospel or put off by it. It is tempting to say that this was the intention of the author. Perhaps on strictly literary-critical grounds one cannot go that far, but should speak only of the implied author. Nevertheless, John's Gospel creates and conveys the impression of a reality that has power to sustain and transform the reader. The text mirrors that reality to the reader.

It reflects a reality distinct from itself or from the reader. Is it also in some sense a window on that reality? Christian theology and proclamation will doubtless go on believing that it is. But a proper appreciation of the character of the Gospel of John requires that it be assessed in its totality and wholeness as a literary work rather than simply being mined or excavated for theological treasure or for historical information, whether about Jesus himself or the circumstances under which it was composed.

CHAPTER TEN

THE TASK OF INTERPRETING THE FOURTH GOSPEL

The interpretation of the Fourth Gospel for preaching must proceed on the basis of an exegetically sound perspective and method. Disciplined analysis and reflection should move back and forth between consideration of what the Gospel meant in antiquity and what it means today. The traditional exegetical question, What did the ancient author intend to say to his readers?, is actually a historical question, and, as we have seen, cannot be answered with absolute certainty. Nevertheless it is still a useful question, and, if asked honestly and without unrealistic expectations, will in the case of John as well as other NT documents prove a guide and a guard against the hazards of historicism on the one hand and allegorical interpretation on the other. Both these hazards, although polar opposites, imperil the exegesis of the Fourth Gospel particularly.

On the one hand, John's portrayal of Jesus and especially his presentation of his words and discourses are often expounded from the pulpit as if they were verbatim historical reports. Such an interpretation, if advanced in all innocence, is understandable and scarcely reprehensible. Nor is it entirely untrue to the intention and purpose of the Gospel, which anchors the presentation of the Christian preaching about Jesus in the preaching and deeds of Jesus. Yet the modern exegete, aware of the great disparity between the synoptic and Johannine portrayals of Jesus, can scarcely regard the Johannine as historical in its departures from the other three. Not only the synoptic Gospels, but also the strands of tradition represented in them (Mark, Q, M, and L), as well as those found in the Didache, the letters of Ignatius, and even the Gospel of Thomas, present a picture of Jesus that is substantially different from the Johannine. The fact that the Johannine Jesus proclaims himself, his messianic dignity and sonship, while as a rule he does not in the other witnesses, also raises serious questions about the historical authenticity of John's representation. One may possibly plead that John supplements the other Gospels or traditions and provides another perspective on Jesus. Although this is certainly true, it is not a consideration which supports the historicity of the Johannine view alongside the others. That the distinctive and characteristic traits of the Johannine portrayal of Jesus should be regarded as having the same, or greater, historical value is scarcely credible. For had Jesus actually spoken in the terms he employs in the Fourth Gospel, it is impossible to understand why the other Gospels and traditions should so little reflect this fact, inasmuch as the faith they too affirm is enunciated by the Johannine Jesus.

At the opposite end of the exegetical spectrum is the temptation to treat the Gospel as a series of symbols or an allegory. That is, of course, understandable in view of the character of the Gospel and the rather negative historical judgments rendered on it in the late nineteenth and early twentieth centuries. Indeed, the symbolic character of the Gospel is obvious, as we have observed. The implied author apparently intends that the reader should appreciate the Gospel's symbolism. Careful and disciplined recognition of the Gospel's symbolism is certainly called for. Moreover, if the Gospel itself becomes at points allegorical, the interpreter must take this into account. Obviously, what is to be avoided is the uncritical flight of the imagination or the importation of a foreign theological agenda. Such treatments of the Gospel were not unheard of in the pre-critical period. Indeed, the earliest known commentary on the Gospel, that of the Valentinian Gnostic Heracleon was apparently of that sort.[63] Moreover, the obvious theological character of the Fourth Gospel may seem to warrant discounting or ignoring any historical question or dimension.

Nevertheless, the historical question presses itself upon us, if not in the old form of whether the Fourth Gospel is an accurate eyewitness report of what Jesus said and did. As has been repeatedly observed, the Evangelist is very much concerned about the historical question in both a broader and narrower sense; broader, in that according to his definition, the history of Jesus does not stop on the date of his crucifixion; narrower, in that he is principally interested only in the Christian theological significance of Jesus' historical ministry. (He is not interested in historical questions generally.) Thus John portrays Jesus in controversy with those who reject the gospel message that he is the Son of God, while comforting, reassuring and supporting those who have come to believe that message and thus are his disciples, his own. His ministry extends into the church's history as a prolongation of the struggle which began in his historical career. The issues have, however, focused or concentrated upon the decisive questions of who he is and what his appearance signifies. That is already an important question for Mark, for the tradition before him, and probably also for the contemporaries and disciples of the historical Jesus. But by John's time, in his community, and in the history of that community's struggle with its Jewish and other rivals, the question of Jesus' identity has been narrowed down and cast in specifically Christian terms. This process of definition and refinement doubtless reflects both developments within and pressures and questions from outside the community. Thus the present Gospel embodies and sets before the reader the history of the preaching, experience, theological questions, and conflicts of what we may now call the Johannine Christian community. An adequate understanding and interpretation of the Fourth Gospel can hardly proceed without an appreciation of this history, although an exact and certain reconstruction of it lies forever beyond our grasp. The Gospel, however, manifests the deep conviction that its presentation of Jesus is in a profound sense historical, in that it accurately states the theological truth of who he was and continues to be.

Thus the question of history and the Fourth Gospel, while a complex one which admits of no simple answer, is not only allowable on the terms posed by the Gospel, but is demanded and pressed upon us. Nevertheless, the historical question really merges into the theological one, for it ultimately becomes the question of whether the history of Jesus, known to us from other traditions (which may be found outside John and also isolated within that Gospel), will in any sense bear the interpretation put upon it. The Evangelist and his school would not only answer affirmatively, but would insist that precisely this interpretation is demanded by history and the tradition when rightly understood.

Interpreting an Interpretation

We are then in the Fourth Gospel confronted with an interpretation, by intention an interpretation of history, not an interpretation that ignores or willingly departs from history. On the one side it is an interpretation, that is, not a chronicle of facts, not history or biography in any ordinary sense of those terms. On the other it is an account, or an accounting, which intends to make the best sense of a history that has become the object of controversy and division. It is a commentary on that history's origin in the light of subsequent reflection and controversy.

Thus, in interpreting the Fourth Gospel we interpret an interpretation. This is, of course, true also in the case of the synoptic Gospels. The difference is simply this: in the synoptics the elements of tradition, many of which are primitive, not yet cast in distinctly Christian terms, often harking back to and representing the historical Jesus *as he actually was,* clearly obtrude in their pristine form and character. In John on the other hand the process of interpretation has gone much farther, or deeper, so that the tradition of Jesus, where it is recognizable at all, has become permeated with the Johannine Christian interpretation of him. This is primarily true of the words and discourses of Jesus, but it is also to some extent true of the narratives, especially the signs, which are recounted in such a way as to underscore the initiative and role of Jesus. The key to an adequate and intellectually or theologically responsible interpretation of John is a recognition of the interpretative character of the narration, which avoids both the Scylla of an impossible historicism bound to yield negative results and the Charybdis of an allegorical, symbolic, or even theological interpretation which simply excludes any consideration of history.

It may be useful at this point to remind ourselves of the three interpretative frames which the Evangelist himself employs in setting Christ forth: the preexistent, eternal; the past, historical; and the present, Christian. Each of these represents his own concern for the historical, but in none, not even the second, does the Gospel remain within purely historical bounds. That is, in no case does the Evangelist limit his presentation to Jesus as he was during his earthly ministry only.

The presentation of Christ as the *pre-existent, cosmic, eternal* Son of God, present with the Father in the beginning and the agent of creation, is scarcely a direct or unavoidable inference from history or historical tradition. Precisely John's portrayal of the rejection of Jesus implies it is not. (Jesus' opponents do not lack the necessary data so much as God-given insight into its meaning.) It is worth observing, however, that John here draws upon a frame of reference and conceptuality found also in other early Christian writings (1 Cor. 8:6; Col. 1:15–17; Heb. 1:2–3); he is not innovating. A minimal and essentially correct assessment of the meaning of this kind of language is that it expresses a need to expand the horizon of history in order to do justice to the significance of the revelatory event that has occurred within it. This assessment is useful as far as it goes, and the modern interpreter may be able to go no farther. He should nevertheless remember that the limitations he is likely to impose on "history" and the "historical" are greatly influenced by, if not derived from, a secular understanding of the historical, according to which just those theological dimensions perceived by the Evangelist are excluded or bracketed out. Yet the modern interpreter or preacher will scarcely be able to deal with the Evangelist's assertions about the pre-existence of Christ, either existentially or metaphysically, except in so far as he is able to see in them an expression of conviction about the ground, origin, validity, and meaning of the gospel of Jesus Christ. And in fact such a perspective does no violence to the intention and linguistic usage of the Evangelist. When in the Gospel John the Baptist says that Jesus was before him (1:15, 30), although he came afterward in temporal sequence, or Jesus says, "Before Abraham was, I am" (8:58), they are clearly using temporal terms to signify something other and more important than sheer time sequence. Jesus' priority in time points to his priority in being, in relationship to God, in the purpose of God, in significance for humanity. So also if Jesus actually appeared after John the Baptist, it can nevertheless be said that he was before him. This larger frame in which John sets his portrait of Jesus invites the interpreter or preacher to expand upon the significance of Christ with reference to the outermost reaches of the conceptual framework of his own day. It challenges him to ask whether he can, in equivalent terms, affirm and proclaim about Jesus what John affirms and proclaims. It lays upon him the task of finding, appropriating, and refining the verbal, conceptual, or other tools by which this may be done.

The *historical framework* of Jesus in the Fourth Gospel is not, of course, confined to a period of three or fewer years at the end of the third decade of the first century, that is, the period of Jesus' earthly ministry. Rather, as we have seen, John merges the history of Jesus into the history of his church, so that Jesus himself becomes the chief protagonist of his disciples and the gospel they preach. To make a rough comparison and generalization, Luke writes his Gospel and puts the Book of Acts alongside or after it; John writes his Gospel and overlays it with an account of his Christian community, particularly its struggles. If one regards the history of Jesus as having no future beyond the date of Jesus' crucifixion, this is an utterly inadmissible, even incomprehensible, procedure. If, on the other hand, one is willing to take John's presuppositions seriously, interesting possibilities or avenues for interpretation open up. John's Gospel presents Jesus' encounter with the questions and issues which have been addressed to his followers by a hostile world, specifically questions which challenge their belief about who he is. The Jewish opponents of Jesus, who in the Gospel expand to become the hostile world, react to the Christian claims about him with incredulity and disbelief. Who is he that such claims should be made for him or folk should be asked to entrust their lives and destinies so fully to him? The question is one whose pertinence is not confined to the latter part of the first Christian century. The answer that Jesus himself gives to that question and challenge is the confession of the Christian community, and particularly of the circles which John represents, and that confession boggles the mind of this world.

Much of the Fourth Gospel conveys the impression that the confrontation between Jesus and his disciples on the one hand and the world on the other leads only to rejection on either side, an absolute standoff. Yet the conviction that faith in Jesus is a possibility given to all people equally seems also to underlie this Gospel (3:16–17; 12:32). God did not send the Son into the world to condemn the world (3:17). What is more, although the world's conversion is not anticipated as the immediate result of the preaching of the gospel, the church's witness to Jesus is to be continued. His disciples are sent into the world by the risen Jesus, just as he was sent (20:21). The witness to the world is a necessity laid upon the church by Jesus himself, whether or not it is successful. The warrant for that ministry and the assurance that it will not be futile are grounded both in its origin and its *raison d'être*. The conclusion of the final prayer of Jesus (17:20–26) suggests the possibility that the witness of the church may bear fruit. The unity of the community will convince the world of Christ's origin in God. If the history of the community is expressed in terms of Jesus' participation in its controversy and struggle, as well as in its consolation and support, the mission of Jesus to the world finds fruition in the community's witness. That witness is not only verbal, but includes the testimony of its inner life, that is, of the relations among its members.

The question raised by the historical dimension of the Fourth Gospel for the interpretive and preaching tasks is not whether the Gospel contains an accurate historical report of Jesus' ministry, but whether and how the continuation of that history in the early Johannine church's preaching and mission is relevant to the present day. The setting of the Fourth Gospel and the Johannine church is not the same as, or even analogous with, the many settings of churches in the modern world. For example, to attempt to translate the Jewish-Christian polemic of the first century into a modern Jewish-Christian polemic would be an extremely unfortunate and unproductive step. Moreover, there are indications that this particular polemical situation is already receding into the past for the Johannine Evangelist and community, as the Jews increasingly become a surrogate for the opposition of the world. John nevertheless places before the interpreter the basic question and challenge of whether and how the history of Jesus, indeed, an ancient Christian theological understanding and appropriation of that history, speaks to the present-day situation of Christians or the church. The historical references to the Jews or Pharisees in terms of which the darkness or the opponents of Jesus are pictured may be obsolete, but the understanding of the relationship of the church to the world reflected therein need not be. It is the intention of John to underline and emphasize the demarcation and difference between faith in Jesus and unbelief. For the Gospel of John everything hinges upon this pivotal point. It is a good question whether one can with integrity preach from John's Gospel if he doubts the continuing centrality of this issue. To join Jesus and his community is the way, and in his view the only way, to come from darkness into light.

For the modern believer or interpreter, beset with the ambiguities of institutional religion on the one hand and of secularity on the other, the question of the identity or identifying marks of that community may prove to be a crucial and difficult one. Just that question was also at issue for the Evangelist: "By this all men will know that you are my disciples, if you have love for one another" (13:35). It is all too easy to see these marks in terms of a facile confession. In John's time the confession was costly, not facile, and the identifying mark was love. Moreover, the insight that the struggle of Jesus against the forces of darkness is continued in the struggle of the church and the world and the corollary conviction that Jesus stands with and within his church in that struggle continue to provide accurate and useful perspectives from which to interpret the Fourth Gospel.

This observation evokes the third and final interpretive framework in which the Fourth Gospel places Jesus. He is *present* as the leader and Lord of his disciples. Of course, we should remind ourselves that in all three dimensions or moments of his reality Jesus is just that. He is, tautologous as it may sound, the *Christian* Christ. That is, he is no longer just the Jewish Messiah, although in the Evangelist's conviction he was that also. As the pre-existent one he is the Christ of the church's confession. As the figure from the past who is represented in the church's historical controversies and struggles he is again the Christ of Christian confession. What then is added by speaking of a third dimension or hermeneutical frame of christological interpretation? First, and perhaps most important, it serves to underscore the Johannine conviction that Jesus is present with his disciples, his church. His present reality is not known just from the past; his past reality is also known from the present. The disciples are not left alone to fend for themselves in the world. Jesus Christ was not only in the beginning and with the church in its infancy and development, he is in the midst of his disciples today; that is, the Evangelist's today. Thus the recent literary-critical approach to John's Gospel is not untrue to its character, for it is an attempt to allow the Evangelist's today to become present to the reader through an appreciation (and appropriation) of his creative work.

For the present-day interpreter there remains the question of how or in what further sense Jesus may be said to continue to abide among his disciples even now. In the Gospel of John his presence is given not only in tradition and memory, nor even in sacrament and institution. In the Spirit-Paraclete and the spiritual experiences of the congregation Jesus makes himself known. Particularly in Spirit-inspired prophecy and prophets the word of Jesus is made known anew among his disciples. He continues to speak. Yet his fundamental command has been made known already in his earthly ministry. He commands his disciples to love one another. This commandment is clearly a central part of the tradition of Jesus, cited as such in the synoptics and 1 John and found also in Paul.[64] No new truth imparted from Jesus through the Spirit can contradict or set aside the love command of Jesus. The fundamental direction and character of the revelation of God in Jesus is given in the historical ministry.

Be that as it may, and it is a very important fact, the Johannine Jesus is also significantly alive among his disciples and his living reality is communicated through the Spirit. For Catholic Christians historically and down to the present day, this abiding and living reality is perhaps imparted primarily sacramentally. For Pentecostals, particularly those involved in some of the newer forms of charismatic Christianity, the Spirit once again mediates the reality of Jesus. As for Protestants, preaching has generally been viewed as the fundamental mode whereby the gospel's reality, if not the presence of the living Christ, is made known and becomes available. While this last view of the matter also has some affinities with Johannine Christianity, the expectation for preaching is ordinarily not of the same intensity as the expectation of the revivification of the revelation of Christ in the church through the Spirit.

The modern interpreter or preacher is in this last hermeneutical framework confronted with the severest challenge to his outlook and assumptions. Whether the kinds of operations of the Spirit anticipated and reflected in the Fourth Gospel can or should be revived in churches today is a good question, and the answer to it by no means obvious. Charismatic phenomena among contemporary Christians pose rather serious problems of church doctrine and order, quite possibly not unlike problems raised by similar phenomena nearly two millennia ago. It is therefore not at all surprising that some conservative

Christians, as well as others, have taken a dim view of charismatic activity. It should be noted in this connection, however, that John says nothing about, and therefore gives no explicit approval to the practice of speaking in tongues. Nor are the ministries of the Paraclete of a personal or private sort. Rather they are for the edification of the entire church. The work of the Spirit as understood in the Fourth Gospel is not entirely analogous to the wide range of phenomena now generally described as charismatic Christianity. Yet there are undeniably points of contact or similarity. Perhaps most significant and noteworthy is the commonly held conviction, based upon experience or a variety of experiences, that Jesus is not just back there in history, or even up there in heaven, but in some tangible, palpable, if not specifiable, sense down here among his true followers on earth, that is, in and with his church. If modern, mainline Protestant Christianity lacks such awareness or experience of the present and living reality of Christ, in this respect at least it is deficient by Johannine standards and perhaps vulnerable to the charge of over-intellectualizing the gospel. Not surprisingly, other Christians have found the possibility of this awareness and experience in Catholic, Pentecostal, and neo-Pentecostal traditions.

Also, in the very recent past and still today, a small but growing number of Christians of diverse confessional traditions testify to having found this present reality of Christ in identifying with suffering or struggling humanity. Whether in the American civil rights movement of the 1960s or in more radical forms of protest and revolutionary thought and action, such Christians seek union with Christ through identity with human causes. It is possible, although not fair, to dismiss their efforts as the mere enhancement of political or social goals with the aura of the gospel. At another level, however, such identification expresses a genuinely religious longing, deep-rooted in the Christian tradition and in the Fourth Gospel, to seek and appropriate in some tangible, meaningful way, and at whatever worldly cost, the living Christ. This dimension and the almost instinctive desire are well-expressed in the famous final paragraph of the English translation of Albert Schweitzer's *Quest of the Historical Jesus:*[65]

> He comes to us as One unknown, without a name, as of old, by the lake-side, He came to those men who knew Him not. He speaks to us the same word: "Follow thou me!" and sets us to the tasks which He has to fulfil for our time. He commands. And to those who obey Him, whether they be wise or simple, He will reveal Himself in the toils, the conflicts, the sufferings which they shall pass through in His fellowship, and, as an ineffable mystery, they shall learn in their own experience Who He is.

Paradoxically, Schweitzer, who criticized nineteenth-century scholarship for smuggling Johannine motifs into the reconstruction of the historical Jesus, here strikes a rather Johannine note himself. For he expresses, albeit through the conceptual terms and ethical orientation of modern, Western man, a rather Johannine view of the modality of Christ's identity and presence.

The Gospel of John Within the New Testament

In the church the interpretation of the Fourth Gospel, and consequently preaching from it, have often been beclouded by the indiscriminate synthesis of Johannine texts and motifs with synoptic. This exegetical error is frequently related to, or of the same species as, the historicism which wants to regard the Johannine narrative as historical report. When it is so regarded, the Johannine narrative can be laid alongside, or combined with synoptic materials which are then also taken to be historical. Of course, an interpreter aware of the gospel criticism of the last three quarters of a century can scarcely regard the synoptics in this way either. Yet while the synoptic Gospels are also Christian theological documents, they do convey a much greater burden of primitive tradition in relatively unalloyed form. Be that as it may, a historically honest exegesis cannot proceed to combine uncritically theological or other motifs from various and different NT documents without regard to their original meaning and function. Even between such closely related Gospels as Matthew and Mark the differing emphases and nuances must be respected. Thus the canons of historical exegesis are badly battered and bent, if not broken completely, when synoptic and Johannine materials and perspectives are merged and their sharp differences blurred.

Having said this, however, we must nevertheless acknowledge another significant factor in biblical and, specifically, Johannine, exegesis. The individual documents of the NT, and, indeed, the OT, stand within the canon of the Christian Bible. There is a sense in which they authorize the church to speak, in that they (and especially the books of the NT) constitute authoritative apostolic witnesses to the origin and character of the faith which the church proclaims. Without such witnesses the church would have no message of salvation. This consideration does not imply that the application of critical exegetical method to the NT is illegitimate or needs to be qualified in practice, although it will at some point have significant implications for interpretation, which must go beyond historical exegesis.

Furthermore, while the message or content of the NT in a very real sense authorizes the church, the NT is itself authorized by the church. That is, if it is true to say without the NT no church, it is also true to say without the church no NT. Historically or temporally the church certainly has priority over the NT. If theologically there is a certain priority on the side of the NT, it is nevertheless true that the very theological character and function of the NT is bestowed upon it by the church. This is particularly the case if by church we mean or include the preaching and message of the gospel of Jesus Christ, which was enunciated to, in, and by the church before it was written down at all.

Therefore, while critical exegetical method may, indeed must, be applied to NT books in a rigorous, uncompromising, and thoroughgoing way, preaching on the basis of the NT is accountable both to the canons of such exegesis and to the status accorded the NT books as scripture of the Christian church. The resolution of the tension implicit in this dual responsibility constitutes a real problem for the contemporary Christian interpreter, especially insofar as he or she is cognizant of the canons and procedures of exegetical science. If such a resolution does not lie in the direction of, for example, merging Johannine and synoptic texts and perspectives in preaching, neither does it lie in ignoring the canonical status of these Gospels, that is, preaching from John as though the other Gospels did not exist or vice versa. Such a procedure, while perhaps exegetically defensible, is theologically questionable. The ancient church and church fathers in their wisdom set John alongside the synoptics and vice versa, so that we might read them all and read them together.

The history and existence of the canon itself affords a valid reason for what might be called *canonical* exegesis. But more than just the presence together of the several writings in one corpus of holy scripture justifies the undertaking. John stands alongside the other Gospels, fourth or last, as it did in most ancient canonical lists. According to the tradition of the early church it was composed last, in the reign of the Emperor Trajan, toward the end of the first century. The position of the Fourth Gospel probably implies something about how it is to be read, that is, with or after the other three. The ancient tradition also implies or even states that John's Gospel was written in cognizance of the others (Clement, Muratorian Fragment, Eusebius). It is arguable that such early traditions are in part apologetic in nature, whereas in fact John wrote without knowledge of the other Gospels or without acknowledging their authority. They explain the existence of a fourth canonical Gospel that differs so markedly from the others. Thus it presupposes the others and is intentionally different because it seeks to supplement or interpret them. Yet there is a significant element of theological truth in these positions, even if they should prove historically untenable. The singular narrative of Jesus' ministry (the term itself is more appropriate to the synoptics) in the Fourth Gospel is to be read after and alongside the synoptic accounts, each of which is much closer to the others than to John. It is then the Jesus who says, "Come to me all who are weary and heavy-laden," who also says, "I am the way and the truth and the life, no one comes to the Father but by me."

The Fourth Gospel is balanced on the other side, so to speak, by the Johannine Epistles. One reads the Fourth Gospel with the other Gospels and also with the letters of John. Its distinctly Johannine portrayal of Jesus as one who knows what is going to happen before it takes place, tells his disciples (before they can know) so that they will also know and understand when it does (13:19; 16:4), performs clearly unprecedented miracles (9:32), and dies by his own volition (10:18), with the Christology that all this implies, is qualified by the synoptic portrayal and by the insistence of the letters that he was really human, really flesh (1 John 1:1–4; 4:1ff.; 2 John 7). Perhaps 1 John's emphasis on the tangibility of Christ (1:2–3) is intended to insure the proper interpretation of the Gospel's simple assertion (1:14) that "the word became flesh and dwelt among us."

On this point Raymond Brown has made an ingenious proposal.[66] The Fourth Gospel was being misconstrued and misinterpreted by some Johannine Christians, who, among other things, did not take such statements as 1:14 to imply the full fleshliness or humanity of Jesus. The First Epistle was then written in part to combat this incipient heresy by insisting on his tangibility and fleshliness, indeed upon the reality of Jesus Christ's death (5:6–8) and its efficacy as an atonement for sin (1:7). It becomes, in effect, a guide to a proper theological, christological understanding of the Gospel. At the same time the other Gospels provide a fuller and more balanced account of Jesus and his ministry. Probably we can never be sure of the historical accuracy of Brown's proposal, or indeed of the exact chronological relationship of the Epistles to the Gospel. But it has at least the advantage of corresponding rather closely to the way in which the letters, especially 1 John, have functioned for the readers of the NT. John 1:14 has generally been construed as carrying the force of 1 John 1:1–4. That John 1:14 must be read that way is, however, less than obvious, particularly if it be granted that the Johannine Epistles are by a different author than the Gospel.

As for the relation to the synoptics, the traditional view that John wrote to supplement and interpret them would, if true, be most convenient for our purposes. There are, as we have at several points observed, some real problems with this position. On the contrary, it can be argued that John wrote without knowledge of the other Gospels or at least without them primarily in view. If John knew Mark or any of the other Gospels, to explain why he treated them as he did, largely ignoring their content even at points where he might have drawn upon them, becomes a major difficulty.

At the same time, literary analysis of the narrative of the Fourth Gospel suggests that it is addressed to readers who are not only informed about the Christian message, but who also know at least important features of the gospel story as we have it in the synoptic Gospels.[67] The initial story of Jesus' encounter with the Baptist does not explicitly mention that Jesus was baptized by him. Yet so many elements of the synoptic (Markan) account are present or alluded to that most readers familiar with the synoptics would assume it and scarcely realize the baptism itself is missing. At the end of Jesus' public ministry, at the beginning of his trial before Pilate, the Jews obviously believe Jesus has committed an offense worthy of death (18:31). Nothing that has been done or said since his arrest warrants that conclusion, although the Jews have been seeking Jesus' life as a blasphemer for a long period at his point in the narrative. In Mark's narrative, however, Jesus' appearance before Pilate is immediately preceded by a trial before the Sanhedrin, at which the high priest (in Matthew explicitly called Caiaphas, as in John) and the council finally proclaim Jesus worthy of death because of his blasphemy. Curiously, John does not have this account, which would have fit his purposes and completed his narrative. After a brief hearing before Annas (who is confusingly also called high priest), Jesus is led to the house of Caiaphas the high priest (18:24) and from there on to Pilate (18:28), but without any indication of what happened when they met. Is it assumed that the reader would know the trial scene we find in Mark and Matthew (but, interestingly, not in exactly the same form or place in Luke)? There is a place for it in John's narrative, and his account of the subsequent trial before Pilate would accommodate it well. Yet it is missing. Is the reader supposed to supply it from Mark or should he understand from the earlier confrontations between Jesus and the Jews that the latter find him guilty of blasphemy?

The implied reader of John knows Jesus already. This may be assumed of the reader in all the Gospels, but Jesus is introduced by the infancy narratives in Matthew and Luke, and by the Baptist in Mark. In John, on the other hand, Jesus Christ is mentioned in 1:17 as if he is known. Although he appears just after the Baptist speaks of the one who comes after him (1:27), as in Mark, Jesus is described in John as one who stands among you, whom you do not know (v. 26). But in the latter instance John the Baptist addresses the Pharisees, who never really know him. The not knowing then applies only to them and not to the Christian reader. Apparently the reader will know Jesus and know of his death and resurrection (2:22), his "hour," which is alluded to frequently in the Fourth Gospel, but not predicted as in the synoptics. Nicodemus, Lazarus, the Beloved Disciple, Annas, Caiaphas and Joseph of Arimathea are introduced as if they are not known to the reader, as is Barabbas, if almost as an afterthought (18:40). Most of the other characters in the Gospel story, however, appear to be known to the implied reader. Notably, Pontius Pilate is not introduced—but neither is he introduced in Mark.

Does the implied reader then know the synoptic Gospels? As we have already seen, this conclusion follows inevitably only if the reader could have known the story by no other means or source. Otherwise, it is not demanded. If John does not know the synoptics, however, or if the implied reader does not know them, they both know some version of the gospel story. In any case, the fact that John follows the synoptics in the NT is not misleading, for the Fourth Gospel does seem to presuppose some such knowledge of Jesus as is conveyed to us through them. But, although the content of John's christological affirmations is not radically different from the synoptics, the weight and emphasis they receive in the narrative surely is. Therefore, the Johannine picture of Jesus and its implications for the nature of Christian interests and the character of Christology really add up to something rather different. If taken by itself John's Jesus, and the Gospel's Christology, look significantly different from the Jesus of Matthew, Mark, or Luke. But that makes all the more intriguing and important the question of whether John's presentation was ever intended to be taken by itself.

Certainly since the second century in the history of exegesis and doctrine the answer to that question has been that John was not intended to be read alone without the accompaniment of the other Gospels. Prior to that, especially at its inception, its intended accompaniment (whether one or more of the synoptics) is much less certain, although the Gospel of John clearly knows more gospel tradition than it conveys (20:30; 21:25). Moreover, if it is correct that John's intense and narrow concentration on Christology, the claims of or for Jesus, arises out of a polemical situation, such a focus on matters directly related to the object of the polemic might be expected. If the implied historical situation of the Fourth Gospel, which we have suggested in some detail, was real and not imaginary, the narrowly focused concentration of the Gospel is easy to understand. Its original intention, as it may then be inferred, was limited—crucially significant for the Johannine community—but limited nevertheless. To read it apart from that historical limitation without regard for that context and the way it has shaped the Gospel would result in an historically distorted, infelicitous, and even dangerous interpretation, one untrue to the Gospels' origin and purpose.

That origin and purpose were in all probability lost, forgotten, or at best obscured when John became a part of the canon of holy scripture. Then the possibility of weighing, assessing, understanding John against its originating environment was lost, although it may well have been restored by modern historical investigation. Nevertheless, this loss was offset in the development of the canon when John was put alongside other Gospels. If John would no longer be read with an understanding of the conflict which shaped it and gave it its distinctive character in the first instance, it would not be read in a vacuum. The historical context would, in effect, be replaced by a literary context, the NT. That context would function in an analogous way, to prevent the claims of, and for, Jesus from being cut off from the *realia* of human existence. Instead of a rather narrowly defined conflict, there would be the broader but not unrelated range of interests and claims that the synoptic Gospels and, indeed, the whole NT reflect or express. Yet the effect would be similar, or potentially so. John's Gospel would once again be understood against the background of the ministry of the historical Jesus and the issues which defined it, and within the matrix of richly manifold tradition which sprang from it. Such an understanding enabled and enables the reader to read the Fourth Gospel in a canonical balance. If the modern reader also reads it in its probable historical context and as a work of literature in its own right, he may well find to his surprise and satisfaction that these different ways of reading the Gospel are amazingly complementary.

John Calvin may have been right when he said that the Fourth Gospel provides the key for understanding the other three.[68] That is to say, the questions which they raise or imply lead to such a christological utterance and confession of faith as is found in the Gospel of John. At the same time, however, one would not want to say that now, having the Fourth Gospel, there is no need for the other three. They pose the questions and issues that make the Fourth Gospel intelligible to us. But they do more than that. They give to Christology and soteriology the kind of rootage in the historical Jesus which would otherwise be lacking. They reflect the realistic humaneness, the more Jewish but also more universal, less uniquely Christian, moral concern and appeal that Jesus doubtless possessed and which the church does well to foster and diffuse. Whether the Gospel of John represents a naive docetism is a question that NT scholars will continue to debate. Probably it is incipiently docetic in at least this sense: If the church had not possessed the other Gospels the forces which in the early centuries and later pulled it in the direction of docetism, Gnosticism, and a false, world-denying spirituality would have almost surely prevailed. In its place, however, that is, in the canon of Christian scriptures, the Fourth Gospel functions in an altogether salutary and necessary way, calling attention to what is uniquely Christian about Jesus.

NOTES

1. See the Ph.D. dissertation of Joseph D. Smith, "Gaius and the Controversy Over the Johannine Literature" (Yale University, 1979). For Smith's demonstration that Gaius' criticisms of the Fourth Gospel were based upon its differences from the synoptics, see 289–92, 368–411.

2. Cf. Eusebius, *Ecclesiastical History* 6.14.7: ". . . John, last of all, conscious that the outward facts had been set forth in the Gospels, was urged on by his disciples, and divinely moved by the Spirit, composed a spiritual Gospel." The phrase "outward facts" is chosen by the Loeb translator J. E. L. Oulton to represent *ta somatika*. See *Eusebius: The Ecclesiastical History,* 2 vols. (Loeb Classical Library; Cambridge: Harvard Univ. Press, 1932), 2:49.

3. Hans Windisch, *Johannes und die Synoptiker,* Untersuchungen zum Neuen Testament, 12 (Leipzig: Hinrichs, 1926). The subtitle is "Did the Fourth Evangelist want to supplement the older Gospels or displace them?". See also E. C. Colwell, *John Defends the Gospel* (Chicago: Willett Clark, 1936), which presupposes John's use of the synoptics as well as his intention to correct them.

4. P. Gardner Smith, *Saint John and the Synoptic Gospels* (Cambridge: Cambridge Univ. Press, 1938).

5. See C. H. Dodd, *Historical Tradition in the Fourth Gospel* (Cambridge: Cambridge Univ. Press, 1963), 8. Cf. Dodd's earlier *The Interpretation of the Fourth Gospel* (Cambridge: Cambridge Univ. Press, 1953), 449. For a more recent discussion, see D. M. Smith, "John and the Synoptics: Some Dimensions of the Problem," *New Testament Studies* 26 (1980): 425–44.

6. Rudolf Bultmann, *The Gospel of John: A Commentary,* trans. G. B. Beasley-Murray et al. (Philadelphia: Westminster Press, 1971), originally published in Germany in 1941.

7. The surviving fragments of the commentary of the second-century Valentinian Gnostic Heracleon are conveniently set forth in English translation by R. M. Grant in *Gnosticism: A Source Book of Heretical Writings from the Early Christian Period* (New York: Harper & Bros., 1961), 195–208. Irenaeus acknowledges that Gnostic heretics, particularly Valentinians, have made much use of John's Gospel (*Against Heresies* 1.7.5; 3.11.7) but he explicitly refutes Gnostic interpretation (1.9.1–3). Indeed, he regards the prologue of the Fourth Gospel, when rightly understood, as decisively anti-Gnostic (3.11.1–6). Irenaeus cites the Fourth Gospel frequently and clearly regards it as on par with the other (synoptic) Gospels, arguing that there must be four authoritative Gospels, no more, no less (3.11.8–9). Moreover, he never tires of quoting John 1:3 against the Gnostics (e.g., 1.22.1; 2.2.5) and places 1:14 alongside 1 John 4:1, 2 as

expressing the same anti-Gnostic, anti-docetic position (3.16.8). Interestingly enough, he sometimes seems to prefer the Johannine narrative account over the synoptic, as, for example, when he bases his view of Jesus' advanced age on John 8:56–57 (2.22.4–6). (*Against Heresies* cited according to the A. Roberts and J. Donaldson edition of *The Ante-Nicene Fathers*.)

8. On the difficulties of the Fourth Gospel in the early church see J. N. Sanders, *The Fourth Gospel in the Early Church: Its Origin and Influence on Christian Theology up to Irenaeus* (Cambridge: Cambridge Univ. Press, 1943), whose position finds support in M. R. Hillmer's dissertation, "The Gospel of John in the Second Century" (Th. D. thesis, The Divinity School, Harvard University, 1966), and in the famous and important work of W. Bauer, *Orthodoxy and Heresy in Early Christianity*, trans. R. A. Kraft and G. Krodel (Philadelphia: Fortress Press, 1971), 187, 206–12. For another viewpoint see F. M. Braun, *Jean le Théologien et son Évangile dans l'Église ancienne*, Études Bibliques 1 (Paris: J. Gabalda, 1959), esp. 65–66.

9. Ernst Käsemann, *The Testament of Jesus: A Study of the Gospel of John in Light of Chapter 17*, trans. Gerhard Krodel (Philadelphia: Fortress Press, 1968), 75.

10. This distinctive emphasis of 1 John was set in clear focus by Hans Conzelmann in a justly famous article, "'Was von Anfang war,'" in *Neutestamentliche Studien für Rudolf Bultmann*, Beihefte zur Zeitschrift fur die neutestamentliche Wissenschaft, vol. 21 (Berlin: Töpelmann, 1954), 194–201.

11. R. E. Brown, *The Epistles of John*, Anchor Bible, vol. 30 (Garden City, N.Y.: Doubleday & Co., 1982).

12. On Paul and John see Bultmann, *Theology of the New Testament*, trans. K. Grobel, 2 vols. (New York: Charles Scribner's Sons, 1955), 2:9: "Clearly, then, John is not of the Pauline school and is not influenced by Paul; he is, instead, a figure with his own originality and stands in an atmosphere of theological thinking different from that of Paul." On the other hand, the "independence of John emerges all the more clearly as one perceives *the deep relatedness in substance that exists between John and Paul* [italics Bultmann's] in spite of all their differences in mode of thought and terminology." Although Albert Schweitzer, *The Mysticism of Paul the Apostle* (New York: Henry Holt, 1931), had assumed John's knowledge of Paul, he poked fun at Deissmann's view of John as an interpreter of Paul (p. 372): "One might as well say that Beethoven was the best interpreter of Bach!"

13. On Bultmann's view of the Gnosticism of John, see *The Gospel of John: A Commentary*, 29–31; on its relation to Qumran and to Judaism generally see *Theology*, 2:13.

14. W. D. Davies, *Paul and Rabbinic Judaism*, 4th ed., rev. (Philadelphia: Fortress Press, 1980) first appeared in 1948, the vanguard of a new approach to Paul and to early Christianity generally.

15. Actually, there are two interpretations, one "christological" (13:6–10) and the other "ethical" (13:12–17).

16. As suggested by R. E. Brown, *The Gospel According to John* (xiii–xxi), Anchor Bible, vol. 29A (Garden City, N.Y.: Doubleday & Co., 1970), 581–604, esp. 582–97. Brown believes chaps 15—16 were added to a discourse originally intended to end at 14:31, but not that they necessarily represent a later perspective.

17. Brown, *The Gospel According to John* (i–xii), 3.

18. The key phrase is translated variously: "the Word was God" (Douay, Jerusalem, KJV, RSV); "what God was, the Word was" (NEB); "the Logos was divine" (Moffatt); and "the Word was divine" (Goodspeed).

19. It is possible that the Greek *katelaben* (RSV, "overcome") in v. 5 should be translated "comprehended," in the sense of "understood." This would make the verse closely parallel to vv. 10 and 11, which apparently refer to Jesus also. It is not impossible that the author realizes the ambiguity of the term and intentionally uses it to convey both meanings.

20. Such a rivalry may also be implied by such passages as Luke 7:18–35 and 11:1, although their tone is by no means so clearly polemical as John's. Followers of John the Baptist continued as a sect within Judaism throughout the first Christian centuries. Acts reports that Paul encountered some disciples of John at Ephesus, who were distinguished from Jesus' followers in that their baptism did not include the gift of the Holy Spirit (Acts 19:1–7). The Mandaean religious movement, which still exists in Iran, holds John the Baptist in high esteem and may have originated from a Baptist sect. See Dodd, *The Interpretation of the Fourth Gospel*, 115–30.

21. See R. Bultmann's article on *aletheia*, etc., in G. Kittel, *Theological Dictionary of the New Testament*, trans. G. Bromiley, et al., 10 vols. (Grand Rapids: Wm. B. Eerdmans, 1964–76), 1:238–251.

22. W. A. Meeks, *The Prophet-King: Moses Traditions and the Johannine Christology,* Supplements to Novum Testamentum, vol. 14 (Leiden: E. J. Brill, 1967), has made a rich and insightful investigation of Jewish traditions about Moses which may have influenced the Fourth Gospel.

23. Both the manuscript evidence and the logic of textual criticism ("Prefer the harder reading or the one which best explains the others.") argue in favor of this reading. Its existence in a very early papyrus manuscript (p66) indicates that it could not have been introduced to combat the later Arian heresy.

24. See G. von Rad, K. G. Kuhn, and W. Gutbrod on *Israel, Hebraios, Ioudaios*, and related terms in Kittel, *Theological Dictionary of the New Testamant*, 3:356–91.

25. Our understanding of the setting of the Gospel of John owes a great deal to the seminal book of J. Louis Martyn, *History and Theology in the Fourth Gospel*, 2d ed., rev. (Nashville: Abingdon Press, 1979), of which the original edition appeared in 1968.

26. See Martyn, *History and Theology in the Fourth Gospel*, esp. 15–62. Cf. Brown, *The Gospel According to John (i–xii),* lxxxv, 374, 379–80.

27. On the motif of Jesus' origin and background in the Fourth Gospel, note several earlier passages: 1:46; 3:31ff; 6:42; 7:15, 27, 41–42, 52; 8:23, 41–42, 57–58.

28. There is an apparent anomaly in this statement of Jesus. For elsewhere it is explicitly said that he does not come in order to judge (3:17–18, where the word *condemn* translates the same Greek word *krino*, "to judge"; also 12:47). From 5:22ff., however, it is clear that the Son does judge. The difficulty is resolved if we see that the ultimate purpose of Jesus' coming is not judgment but salvation (3:16ff.). Yet from this, judgment inevitably results, because some reject with great hostility the salvation that is offered and persist in evil (3:19ff.). This negative statement of Jesus' purpose is doubtless influenced by the context, as it follows a narrative in which hostility toward Jesus and his work has been vigorously expressed.

29. See Martyn, *History and Theology in the Fourth Gospel*, 66–67, 72ff., esp. 80–81, for the view that passages such as 5:18 (cf. 7:19; 8:59; 10:31) indicate that Christian believers in the synagogue were in danger of legal processes possibly culminating in execution. On the other hand, Douglas R. A. Hare, *The Theme of Jewish Persecution of Christians in the Gospel According to Matthew,* Society for New Testament Studies Monograph Series, vol. 6 (Cambridge: Cambridge Univ. Press, 1967), 20–43, examines the NT and other early evidence and concludes that while a few Christians such as Stephen were undoubtedly killed by Jews their deaths were the results of mob action, i.e., lynching, rather than judicial process. He observes that in the later NT books (1 Timothy to Revelation) and in the Apostolic Fathers there are no reported instances of Christians being put to death by Jews (p. 43, n. 1). In any event, the difference of opinion is over the question of the legal, or extra-legal, character of instances in which Christians were killed by Jewish antagonists.

30. The underlying social basis for the theological conceptuality or ideology of John is explored by Wayne A. Meeks in a pioneering article, "The Man from Heaven in Johannine Sectarianism," *Journal of Biblical Literature* 91 (1972): 44–72.

31. On the meaning of the term one should consult the standard lexical work of W. Bauer, *A Greek-English Lexicon of the New Testament and Other Early Christian Literature*, trans. W. F. Arndt and F. W. Gingrich, 2d ed., rev. by Gingrich and F. W. Danker (Chicago: Univ. of Chicago Press, 1979), as well as the article *"Parakletos"* by J. Behm in Kittel, *Theological Dictionary of the New Testament*, 5:800–814.

32. The close relationship between the Paraclete and Jesus has been rightly emphasized by R. E. Brown, "The Paraclete in the Fourth Gospel," *New Testament Studies* 13 (1967): 113–32.

33. Cf. G. Johnston, *The Spirit-Paraclete in the Gospel of John*, Society for New Testament Studies Monograph Series, vol. 12 (Cambridge: Cambridge Univ. Press, 1970), who links the Gospel and the Evangelist with such Spirit-inspired prophecy (119, 126).

34. Cf. W. Wrede, *The Messianic Secret*, trans. J. C. G. Greig (Cambridge: James Clarke, 1971), 181–210. See esp. 186: "We can accordingly be in no doubt about John's having a view closely related to that of Mark in regard to the disciples' recognition of Jesus. In this it is of value to note that he expressly singles out the resurrection as the decisive moment in time." Cf. also 204ff.

35. This insight is, of course, derived from the significant and stimulating work of J. Louis Martyn, *History and Theology in the Fourth Gospel*, who posits two levels of historical narration in John's accounts of Jesus' deeds and discourses.

36. Cf. F. Mussner, *The Historical Jesus in the Gospel of John*, trans. W. J. O'Hara (Freiburg: Herder, 1967), 17: ". . . in the development of theology, John faced the hermeneutical task of 'understanding' Jesus. . . . Understanding of Jesus was for John primarily an *historical knowledge*." Also 46–47: ". . . Jesus of Nazareth is so expressed by John in his act of vision that the history of Christ projected and presented by him simultaneously gives an answer to the Christological questions of the time of its composition. This answer is not, however, obtained by speculation about the mystery of Jesus, but precisely by that retrospective gaze which the act of vision makes possible. . . . Retrospection is not a mechanical reproduction of the history of Jesus, and in the

act of vision there occurs the exposition effected by the Spirit, and so the historical Jesus becomes the Christ of kerygma, who precisely as such is also the Jesus of history. For 'history' in the proper sense is of course 'history as operative influence.'"

37. The three relevant decrees were issued on May 29, 1907. See A. Robert and A. Feuillet, *Introduction to the New Testament*, trans. P. W. Skehan et al. (New York: Desclee, 1965), 606–7. Raymond F. Collins, *Introduction to the New Testament* (Garden City, N.Y.: Doubleday & Co., 1983), 356–86, gives a helpful overview of "Rome and the Critical Study of the New Testament."

38. See Bultmann's *The Gospel of John*, passim, and cf. D. M. Smith, *The Composition and Order of the Fourth Gospel: Bultmann's Literary Theory*, Yale Publications in Religion, vol. 10 (New Haven: Yale Univ. Press, 1965), passim, and esp. xi–xv.

39. C. H. Dodd, "The First Epistle of John and the Fourth Gospel," *Bulletin of the John Rylands Library* 21 (1937): 129–56, first made the case for separate authorship on stylistic and conceptual grounds. There followed the brief but significant article of H. Conzelmann, "Was von Anfang war," in *Neutestamentliche Studien für Rudolf Bultmann*, 194–201, in which he pointed to the significant shift in the meaning of *arche* from Gospel (pre-existence of logos) to First Epistle (beginning of the tradition) as typical of the distinguishing churchly, traditional interests of the author of the Epistle. Conzelmann's insights have been further developed by Günter Klein, "Das wahre Licht scheint schon—Beobachtungen zur Zeit und Geschichtserfahrung einer urchristlichen Schule," *Zeitschrift für Theologie und Kirche* 68 (1971): 261–326.

40. See R. E. Brown, *The Community of the Beloved Disciple* (New York: Paulist Press, 1979), 31–34; also R. Schnackenburg, "On the Origin of the Fourth Gospel" in *Jesus and Man's Hope*, 2 vols. (Pittsburgh: Pittsburgh Theological Seminary, 1970), 1:233–46, esp. 233–43; and Thorwald Lorenzen, *Der Lieblingsjünger im Johannesevangelium: eine Redaktionsgeschichtliche Studie*, Stuttgarter Bibelstudien, vol. 55 (Stuttgart: Katholisches Bibelwerk, 1971), who finds that the Beloved Disciple appears in passages that are compositions of the Evangelist, but nevertheless regards him as a historical figure.

41. So J. Louis Martyn, see n. 25 above. Also see Brown, *The Gospel According to John (i–xii)*, lxxxv. Steven T. Katz, "Issues in the Separation of Judaism and Christianity after 70 C.E.: A Reconsideration," *Journal of Biblical Literature* 103 (1984): 43–76, has strongly contested the relevance of the *Birkat ha-Minim* to the separation of Judaism and Christianity.

42. As to the place of origin, there is no agreement among scholars. The ancient tradition of an Ephesian origin may be correct as far as final composition and publication are concerned. The origin of the Johannine tradition, however, probably lies to the east, in Palestine or Syria. A minority opinion favors Egypt as the locus of the Fourth Gospel. Raymond E. Brown, *The Epistles of John*, 102–3, thinks the evidence suggests a movement of the Johannine community from Palestine to Ephesus.

43. This is, generally, the position of Martyn, *History and Theology in the Fourth Gospel*. A similar and related view, with a highly developed and meticulously argued source theory, has been put forward by R. T. Fortna, *The Gospel of Signs: A Reconstruction of the Narrative Source Underlying the Fourth Gospel*, Society for New Testament Studies Monograph Series, vol. 11 (Cambridge: Cambridge Univ. Press,

1970). Fortna thinks the present Gospel is based upon an earlier narration of Jesus' signs, passion, and resurrection which was used as a missionary tract among Jews.

44. Cf. Meeks, "The Man from Heaven."

45. Such a viewpoint is represented most influentially in the important work of E. Käsemann, *The Testament of Jesus*, see esp. 36ff. Cf. Alv Kragerud, *Der Lieblingsjünger im Johannesevangelium* (Oslo: Osloer Universitäts Verlag, 1959), esp. 93-112, to whom Käsemann refers with reservations (38).

46. The position that the controversies reflected in the Johannine Epistles took place among "Johannine" Christians is set forth and elaborated in detail by Raymond E. Brown, *The Community of the Beloved Disciple*, 93-144, and his Anchor Bible commentary, *The Epistles of John*, passim.

47. *Webster's New International Dictionary of the English Language*, 2d ed. unabridged (Springfield, Mass.: G. & C. Merriam, 1947).

48. R. A. Culpepper, *The Johannine School: An Evaluation of the Johannine-School Hypothesis Based on an Investigation of the Nature of Ancient Schools*, Society of Biblical Literature Dissertation Series, vol. 26 (Missoula, Mont.: Scholars Press, 1975), 258-59; cf. 288-89.

49. For the view that John drew upon Paul, see, e.g., Albert Barnett, *Paul Becomes a Literary Influence* (Chicago: Univ. of Chicago Press, 1941), 104-42, esp. 104-5.

50. See n. 4.

51. See n. 43.

52. Such a purpose has been advocated in recent years by T. C. Smith, *Jesus in the Gospel of John* (Nashville: Broadman, 1959); J. A. T. Robinson, "The Destination and Purpose of St. John's Gospel," *New Testament Studies* 6 (1960): 117-31, and "The Destination and Purpose of the Johannine Epistles," ibid., 7 (1960): 56-65; W. C. Van Unnik, "The Purpose of St. John's Gospel," in *Studia Evangelica: Papers Presented to the International Congress on The Four Gospels in 1957*, ed. K. Aland et al., Texte und Untersuchungen, 73 (Berlin: Akademie Verlag, 1959), 382-411.

53. See Meeks, *The Prophet King*, 216-57, and C. H. H. Scobie, "The Origins and Development of Samaritan Christianity," *New Testament Studies* 19 (1973): 390-415, esp. 401-8.

54. Cf. C. K. Barrett, *The Gospel of John and Judaism*, trans. D. M. Smith (London: SPCK, 1975), 65-69.

55. See, for example, Charles H. Talbert, *What is a Gospel? The Genre of the Canonical Gospels* (Philadelphia: Fortress Press, 1977); also George A. Kennedy, *New Testament Interpretation Through Rhetorical Criticism*, Studies in Religion (Chapel Hill: Univ. of North Carolina Press, 1984), 96-113.

56. R. Alan Culpepper, *Anatomy of the Fourth Gospel: A Study in Literary Design*, Foundations and Facets: New Testament (Philadelphia: Fortress Press, 1983), x.

57. Ibid., 3-5. Our discussion of this and other literary aspects of the Fourth Gospel leans heavily upon Culpepper's basic work.

58. Ibid., 72.

59. Ibid., 56.

60. Ibid., 103.

61. This point was decisively demonstrated at the beginning of the century by two

scholars whose estimates of the character and historical value of the Gospel narratives differed diametrically: Albert Schweitzer, *The Quest of the Historical Jesus*, trans. W. Montgomery (New York: Macmillan Co., 1954), and Wrede, *The Messianic Secret*.

62. Culpepper, *Anatomy*, 163.

63. See R. M. Grant, *Gnosticism*, 195–208.

64. See now V. P. Furnish, *The Love Command in the New Testament* (Nashville: Abingdon Press, 1972), for a comprehensive treatment dealing separately with the several major NT books or traditions.

65. Schweitzer, *Quest of the Historical Jesus*, 403.

66. See n. 46 above.

67. Cf. Culpepper, *Anatomy*, 224.

68. John Calvin, *Commentary on the Gospel According to John*, trans. W. Pringle (Edinburgh: Calvin Translation Society, 1847), 22: ". . . I am accustomed to say that this Gospel is a key to open the door for understanding the rest; for whoever shall understand the power of Christ, as it is here strikingly portrayed, will afterwards read with advantage what the others relate about the Redeemer who was manifested."

SELECTED BIBLIOGRAPHY

I. Commentaries

Good commentaries on the Gospel of John are not in short supply. The following list includes the most significant ones and is otherwise representative.

Barrett, C. K. *The Gospel According to St. John: An Introduction with Commentary and Notes on the Greek Text*. 2d rev. ed. Philadelphia: Westminster Press, 1978. Probably the most useful commentary on the Greek text, and a good commentary by any standard.

Brown, Raymond E. *The Gospel According to John: Introduction, Translation and Notes*. Anchor Bible. 2 vols. Garden City, N.Y.: Doubleday & Co., 1966, 1970. A reliable, thorough, and judicious work. The interpretive commentary upon the substance of the text is as extensive and valuable as the detailed notes.

Bultmann, Rudolf. *The Gospel of John: A Commentary*, trans. G. R. Beasley-Murray et al. Philadelphia: Westminster Press, 1971 (based upon the 1968 German edition). Bultmann's magnum opus on John, which had to wait thirty years after its appearance in 1941 for translation, is a landmark of interpretation and probably the most significant critical commentary of the century.

Haenchen, Ernst. *John 1: A Commentary on the Gospel of John Chapters 1−6* and *John 2: A Commentary on the Gospel of John Chapters 7−21*, trans. Robert W. Funk., Ulrich Busse. Hermeneia. Philadelphia: Fortress Press, 1984. Published from manuscripts on which the author was working at the time of his death, this commentary is understandably thin in spots. Nevertheless, it is full of Haenchen's valuable insights.

Lindars, Barnabas. *The Gospel of John*. New Century Bible Commentary. Grand Rapids: Wm. B. Eerdmans, 1972. A sound and helpful one-volume commentary, typical of the useful series of which it is a part.

Macrae, George. *Invitation to John: A Commentary on the Gospel of John with Complete Text from the Jerusalem Bible*. Garden City, N.Y.: Image Books (Doubleday), 1978. A good, brief commentary, simple and to the point, aimed at a lay audience.

Morris, Leon. *The Gospel According to John: The English Text with Introduction, Exposition and Notes*. The New International Commentary on the New Testament. Grand Rapids: Wm. B. Eerdmans, 1971. The fullest and best recent commentary written from a conservative standpoint.

Sanders, J. N. *A Commentary on the Gospel According to St. John*. Ed. and completed by B. A. Mastin. Harper's New Testament Commentaries. New York: Harper & Row, 1968.

Schnackenburg, Rudolf. *The Gospel According to John*, 3 vols., trans. Kevin Smyth et al. New York: Crossroad, 1968–82. A weighty and significant commentary which reflects the author's developing positions over the decade and a half during which it was composed.

II. Other Important Books and General Studies

Brown, Raymond E. *The Community of the Beloved Disciple.* New York: Paulist Press, 1979. A fascinating thesis regarding the distinctive Christian circles which produced the Johannine literature, their development and dissolution.

Culpepper, R. Alan. *Anatomy of the Fourth Gospel: A Study in Literary Design.* Foundations and Facets: New Testament. Philadelphia: Fortress Press, 1983. An important new approach to the Fourth Gospel based on literary critical insights and perspectives developed from the general analysis of narrative texts.

Dodd, C. H. *Historical Traditions in the Fourth Gospel.* Cambridge: Cambridge Univ. Press, 1963. Published a decade after his earlier work, this widely heralded book seeks to establish the traditional and historical basis of the Johannine narrative independent of the synoptic Gospels. Dodd is more successful in demonstrating the independence of the Johannine tradition than in establishing its historical character.

———. *The Interpretation of the Fourth Gospel.* Cambridge: Cambridge Univ. Press, 1953. A technical and still important study of the background and theology of the Gospel.

Fortna, Robert T. *The Gospel of Signs: A Reconstruction of the Narrative Source Underlying the Fourth Gospel.* SNTS Monograph Series 11. Cambridge: Cambridge Univ. Press, 1970. A thoroughgoing source-critical analysis based on the Greek text.

Käsemann, E. *The Testament of Jesus: A Study of the Gospel of John in the Light of Chapter 17,* trans. G. Krodel. Philadelphia: Fortress Press, 1968; German original, 1966. An incisive presentation of the historical position of John in the light of its theology; Käsemann believes John was influenced by Gnosticism and regards its Christology as incipiently docetic.

Kysar, Robert. *The Fourth Evangelist and His Gospel: An Examination of Contemporary Scholarship.* Minneapolis: Augsburg, 1975. This critical survey of two recent decades of Johannine scholarship affords a good introduction to the problems, issues, and areas of research on which scholars are still at work.

Malatesta, Edward. *St. John's Gospel 1920–1965: A Cumulative and Classified Bibliography.* Analecta Biblica 32. Rome: Pontifical Institute, 1967. The most extensive bibliography, although it is now two decades old.

Martyn, J. Louis. *History and Theology in the Fourth Gospel.* 2d rev. ed. Nashville: Abingdon Press, 1979. An extremely influential effort to fix the historic position of the Gospel of John in relation to Jewish-Christian controversy toward the end of the first century. While aspects of Martyn's thesis are debatable, its general thrust has achieved wide acceptance.

Smith, D. Moody. *Johannine Christianity: Essays on Its Setting, Sources, and Theology.* Columbia, S.C.: Univ. of South Carolina Press, 1984.

III. Commentaries on the Johannine Epistles

Brown, Raymond E. *The Epistles of John: Translated With Introduction, Notes and Commentary.* Anchor Bible 30. Garden City, N.Y.: Doubleday & Co., 1982. The

128   *SELECTED BIBLIOGRAPHY*

definitive commentary on the Letters of John. The thesis set forth in *Community of the Beloved Disciple* is here given thorough exegetical undergirding.

Bultmann, Rudolf. *The Johannine Epistles*, trans. R. P. O'Hara et al. Hermeneia. Philadelphia: Fortress Press, 1973; German original, 1967.

Dodd, C. H. *The Johannine Epistles*. Moffatt New Testament Commentary. London: Hodder and Stoughton, 1946.

Grayston, Kenneth. *The Johannine Epistles*. New Century Bible Commentary. Grand Rapids: Wm. B. Eerdmans, 1984. In opposition to the more commonly held position, Grayston argues that certain primitive aspects of the Epistles, especially 1 John, indicate they were written earlier than the Gospel.

Houlden, J. L. *The Johannine Epistles*. Harper's New Testament Commentaries. New York: Harper & Row, 1973.

Marshall, I. Howard. *The Epistles of John*. The New International Critical Commentary on the New Testament. Grand Rapids: Wm. B. Eerdmans, 1978.

Smalley, Stephen S. *1, 2, 3 John*. Word Biblical Commentary. Waco, Texas: Word Books, 1985. The most recent commentary on the Greek text of the Epistles.

INDEX OF BIBLICAL PASSAGES

INDEX OF ANCIENT AUTHORS AND TEXTS